FOREWORD
by Louis Cassels

Senior Editor
For the Editors of United Press International

At a dark moment in history, near the end of the long night of World War II and just before the dawn of the nuclear age, an unsuccessful haberdasher from Independence, Missouri, suddenly inherited the leadership of the United States and the free world.

He had little preparation for the awesome responsibilities that were so abruptly thrust upon him. But he did have courage, humility, determination and a remarkable capacity for growth. To the surprise of nearly everyone, including himself, he soon emerged from the shadow of his dynamic predecessor, Franklin D. Roosevelt, and became a strong and forceful President in his own right.

His name was Harry S. Truman. He served as President of the United States from April, 1945 until January, 1953—a period of nearly eight years. They were among the most momentous years in America's history. A great war ended, a peace of sorts was made, the nation painfully readjusted to a peacetime economy. A terrifying new weapon—the atomic bomb—took its place in the military arsenal and in the nightmares of all mankind. International Communism, under the aegis of Soviet Russia, mounted an aggressive challenge to the security of free nations. New alliances were formed, new commitments undertaken, on a scale unprecedented in any previous administration. Fidelity to one of these commitments led the United States into a long, costly, undeclared war in Korea.

During his years in the White House, President Truman was the target of a good deal of harsh criticism. Some disapproved of his foreign policy decisions. Others protested the domestic programs through which he sought a "Fair Deal" for the underprivileged. Many simply disliked his style as a man: they found him too earthy, even crude.

Mr. Truman viewed the criticism directed at him with philosophical resignation. It was, he said, part of the heat one had to expect when one ventured into the kitchen of the Presidency. But all Presidents hope to be vindicated by history, and Harry S. Truman, an avid student of history, cared more than most.

It was a signal blessing that he lived long enough to be comfortably certain about the verdict of history. During the nineteen years that elapsed between his retirement from the Presidency and his death, he ceased to be a controversial figure. Even his erstwhile critics acknowledged the far-sightedness and courage of some of the difficult decisions he made as President. And the only debate among historians was whether he should be ranked among America's good Presidents, or elevated to the small circle of great Presidents.

Harry S. Truman died December 26, 1972, at the age of 88. He would have loved reading his obituaries, although he doubtless would have had some waspish comments to make about the eulogies lavished on him by former political enemies.

It was a fitting finale to one of the great success stories of American history. That story is told, in words and pictures, in the pages that follow.

a pictorial biography

HST

TEXT BY DAVID S. THOMSON

GROSSET & DUNLAP, INC.
A NATIONAL GENERAL COMPANY
PUBLISHERS • NEW YORK

1

2

3

4

5

6

7

8

Copyright © 1973 by Grosset & Dunlap, Inc.
All rights reserved
Published simultaneously in Canada
Library of Congress Catalog Card No. 70-164475
ISBN: 0-448-03141-8
ISBN: 0-448-02213-3 (pbk)
First printing
Printed in the United States of America

CONTENTS

AN EBULLIENT PRESIDENT'S GREAT TRIUMPH: ELECTION 1948

In a letter President Harry S. Truman once addressed to his daughter Margaret, he retold a favorite Truman anecdote. "There is an epitaph," he wrote, "in Boothill Cemetery in Tombstone, Arizona, which reads, 'Here lies Jack Williams; he done his damndest.'" Then the President added, "What more can a person do?"

In the nearly eight years that he served as the 33rd President of the United States Harry Truman without question did do his "damndest" to lead the nation wisely, energetically, forcefully. He approached the job of the Presidency with remarkable zeal and great courage. Historians have concluded almost unanimously that he deserves to be ranked as a "near-great" President. Conceivably in years to come, when time has lent further perspective, historians may forego their hedging and let Truman stand forth as a truly "great" Chief Executive.

His qualities of zeal, courage, doing his "damndest" revealed themselves throughout Truman's life: as a boy growing up in a semi-frontier Missouri, as a combat officer in World War I, as a rigidly honest local politician, as a U.S. Senator. He showed these qualities in the forceful way he took hold of the reins of government when he was suddenly catapulted into the Presidency on the death of Franklin D. Roosevelt in 1945. He showed them again and again in meeting a tangled and endless succession of problems—from strikes at home to the Korean War—that beset his Administrations.

Never did Harry Truman exhibit more dramatically his enthusiasm and toughness, however, than in the Presidential campaign of 1948. He was unquestionably the underdog. Nobody, not even his closest friends and advisers, gave Truman a chance of beating the Republican candidate, Governor Thomas E. Dewey of New York. At the time, everything seemed to be going against Truman. Strikes, rising prices and a post-World War II housing shortage were but a few of his domestic problems. In foreign affairs there was the Cold War with an increasingly bellicose Soviet Union—a profoundly disillusioning state of affairs for the American people, who had believed that once Nazi Germany and the Empire of Japan were defeated, the world would enter on an era of universal peace and good will.

A chipper, smiling Truman swings down from his railroad car during his marathon whistle-stop campaign in 1948.

"*The principal quality about Truman that comes to mind is the essential one of vitality. Here is a man overflowing with life force, with incurable curiosity. He's no brooding image in a history book, depressed by the foibles and the misfortunes of life; he is vigorous, powerful, gay, full of the zest of living. He is too much interested in what's ahead to deplore what is past.*" —Dean Acheson

Truman had struggled boldly with these and other problems during the years since he had succeeded Roosevelt. Only four days after the Japanese had signed the surrender aboard the battleship *Missouri*, he was ready with a far-reaching 21-point message to Congress asking for legislation he felt was needed to cope with postwar conditions. It included proposals for an increased minimum wage and federal aid to education. Congressional conservatives, snorting with rage at finding Truman's measures more liberal than those that Roosevelt had proposed, shot down most of the President's program.

"To err is Truman" Even more discouraging was public reaction. Large segments of the population, far from appreciating Truman's efforts, did not even seem to be aware of them. Doubtless this was due, in part at least, to the nation's press, which overwhelmingly favored the Republicans. The papers not only cast a critical eye on all of Truman's political moves; they also jumped gleefully on his blunders and his occasional unguarded statements. Some of his errors were serious. He bungled badly, for example, his handling of the 1946 railroad strike *(pages 86-87)*. But even relatively harmless slips—such as taking a hand in a poker game at a Democratic outing—were trumpeted in the newspapers to prove Truman's lack of fitness for the job. "To err is Truman" became a common jape of the day.

Part of the trouble was H.S.T.'s image. Roosevelt had seemed a reassuringly fatherly figure, sympathetic but somewhat aloof. Truman seemed too jaunty and friendly, his grin too wide. Roosevelt loved jokes and was a hearty laugher, and when aroused could swear with authenticity, but he did these things in private. Truman could not hide his love of horseplay and wisecracks, and he occasionally used Missouri muleskinners' language in public. Roosevelt was tall; Truman, despite his above average height of five feet, nine inches, was always described in the press as a "small man." Somehow, he seemed to lack the dignity required of a President. His direct personality showed through—to his disadvantage.

Combining a generally morose view of Truman's character with the problems he faced, the American people decided that the nation was bumping along over a very rocky road. Many did not stop to ponder that a majority of the problems grew from unavoidable postwar dislocations. Inevitably many laid full blame, as Americans often do, on the doorstep of the President. As the 1948 election approached Truman's chances of remaining in the White House appeared to be zero. Public opinion polls, such as the one conducted by Dr. George Gallup, showed that H.S.T.'s popularity had slipped alarmingly. The press was equally negative. Gloom enveloped the Democratic Party, and rebellious noises were heard. Colonel Jacob "Jake" Arvey, the powerful Democratic boss of Chicago, along with a number of other professional politicians, talked openly and noisily of "dumping" Truman and nominating someone else at the party's convention in July. Some of them approached General Dwight Eisenhower to see if he would consider accepting the nomination. Since Eisenhower, as a military man, could take no official political stance, nobody could tell whether his sympathies were Republican or Democratic. Eisenhower refused the Democrats' overtures, but the search for someone to take Truman's place went on amid growing dissension. The once tight-knit Democratic Party seemed to be tearing itself apart.

It was at this point that Truman, perhaps more than at any other time in his life, showed his courage, his determination—and his appetite, if a fight had to take place, for a good rousing battle. He was not going to be routed from his leadership of the Democratic Party. And he was not going to lose to the Republicans either. He wanted desperately to be elected President in his own right and not go down in history merely as Roosevelt's heir. He wanted to carry on his policies and prove them right, the more so because both he and they had been so harshly attacked. He wanted to carry on the liberal policies of the New Deal because he was convinced they were good for the country.

So Truman set out on one of the most extensive, exhausting, amazing—and ultimately triumphant—election campaigns in American history. On June 3 he boarded a special train and traveled all the way to the West Coast and back. Ostensibly he made the trip to accept an honorary degree at the University of California. Not yet his party's candidate, he could not campaign officially, and his aides billed the trip as "nonpolitical." But it was, of course, wholly political— Truman gave dozens of speeches en route—and it was by and large a rousing success. There was a new fire in Truman's speeches, many delivered extemporaneously, and a new rapport between the President and his audience. As the news got around that H.S.T. was, in the words of one reporter, "a scrappy fighter making an uphill fight," the crowds got larger and more demonstrative.

In Albuquerque came the incident that was to give Truman's campaign its enduring label. As he lashed into the Republican 80th Congress for refusing to enact his legislation, a listener suddenly shouted, "Lay it on, Harry! Give 'em hell!" Truman instantly shot back, "I will! I intend to!" The "Give 'em hell!" campaign was launched and its pattern set. Thereafter Truman, having used his power as President and party chief to get the nomination in July, "whistle-stopped" across much of the nation, making as many as 16 speeches a day, addressing perhaps 15 million people in all. Although the election's outcome was uncertain until the morning after the polls closed, Truman's victory was impressive. The campaign's success justified Truman's faith that if he went directly to the people and explained the issues in plain language he would win.

"Lay it on, Harry! Give 'em hell!"

The sources of this faith and of Truman's amazing determination lay deep within the man and, in a sense, deep within the nation. For Truman shared that basic, simple but pervasive American belief that given enough energy, courage and hard work *anything*, however difficult, can be accomplished. Philosophical observers of the U.S. scene have often noted that Americans characteristically lack the sense, shared by many Europeans, that life is essentially tragic. When something, be it the plumbing or the government, breaks down, Americans typically do not say, "Well, that's life." Instead they try to fix the trouble, and then try to improve the system or the machine so that it will not break down again. In sharing this ingrained optimism, as in so many other ways, Truman showed himself throughout his career to be the archetypal American. "I have never seen pessimists make anything work, or contribute anything of lasting value," he once said. As a youth, as a farmer, as a young politician, as a Senator, as President, Truman always clung to their faith that through sheer hard work and inflexible determination any trouble could be overcome and things of "lasting value" accomplished. Not the least of these things was his astonishing victory in 1948.

STIRRING TURN-OUTS IN THE SMALL TOWNS

President Truman's main weapon in his fight for re-election was the 15-minute speech from the back platform of a special loudspeaker-equipped Pullman car. The train would pull into a town, Truman would speak, invite questions and then close the show by introducing "the boss," his wife Bess, and Margaret. Truman's images were sometimes vivid, not to say violent. "This Republican Congress," he told one Midwest audience, "has already stuck a pitchfork in the farmer's back." He reminded his audiences of the Great Depression and warned that if the people "let this same gang get control of the government" another depression would surely follow. Some of Truman's advisers winced at such language, but it was effective, and it won votes.

President Truman, speaking from the observation platform at the rear of his campaign train *(right)*, addresses a sea of upturned faces at Logansport, Indiana. This turn-out, estimated at 12,000, was typical of the crowds that greeted the President during his second major whistle-stopping trip. His audiences, such as the one shown above, were always attentive but generally undemonstrative.

Attracted by the gathering momentum of Truman's campaign, a crowd clusters atop a boxcar near a giant grain elevator *(left)* to get a better view of the train. At every stop reporters like those hunkering down by the tracks at right struggled to record Truman's latest slam at the Republicans. In the campaign's whirlwind pace, Truman himself never faltered, seeming to draw fresh energy from the direct and jovial give-and-take he established with the people *(below)*.

66 *When the crowds in Pocatello and Sedalia yell 'Tell it, Harry' and 'Pour it on 'em, Harry,' the President warms to his task. 'Oh, I'm pouring it on and I'm going to keep pouring it on,' he cries, in language the people understand.* 99 —Win Booth, a reporter on Truman's train

BUILDING THE CRUCIAL MOMENTUM

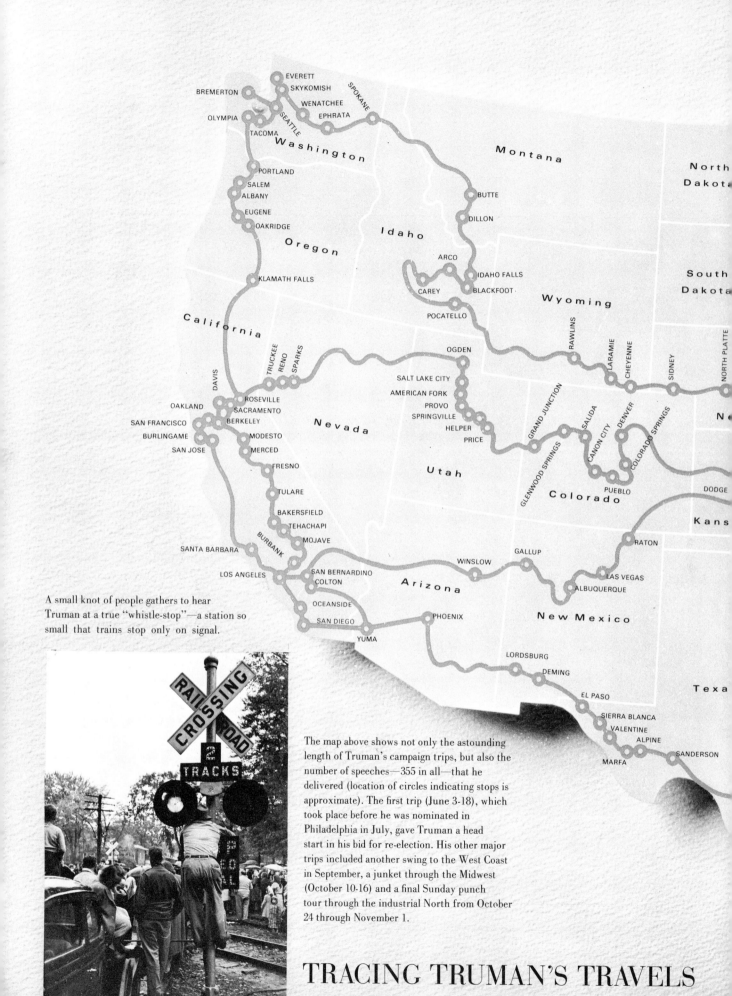

A small knot of people gathers to hear Truman at a true "whistle-stop"—a station so small that trains stop only on signal.

The map above shows not only the astounding length of Truman's campaign trips, but also the number of speeches—355 in all—that he delivered (location of circles indicating stops is approximate). The first trip (June 3-18), which took place before he was nominated in Philadelphia in July, gave Truman a head start in his bid for re-election. His other major trips included another swing to the West Coast in September, a junket through the Midwest (October 10-16) and a final Sunday punch tour through the industrial North from October 24 through November 1.

TRACING TRUMAN'S TRAVELS

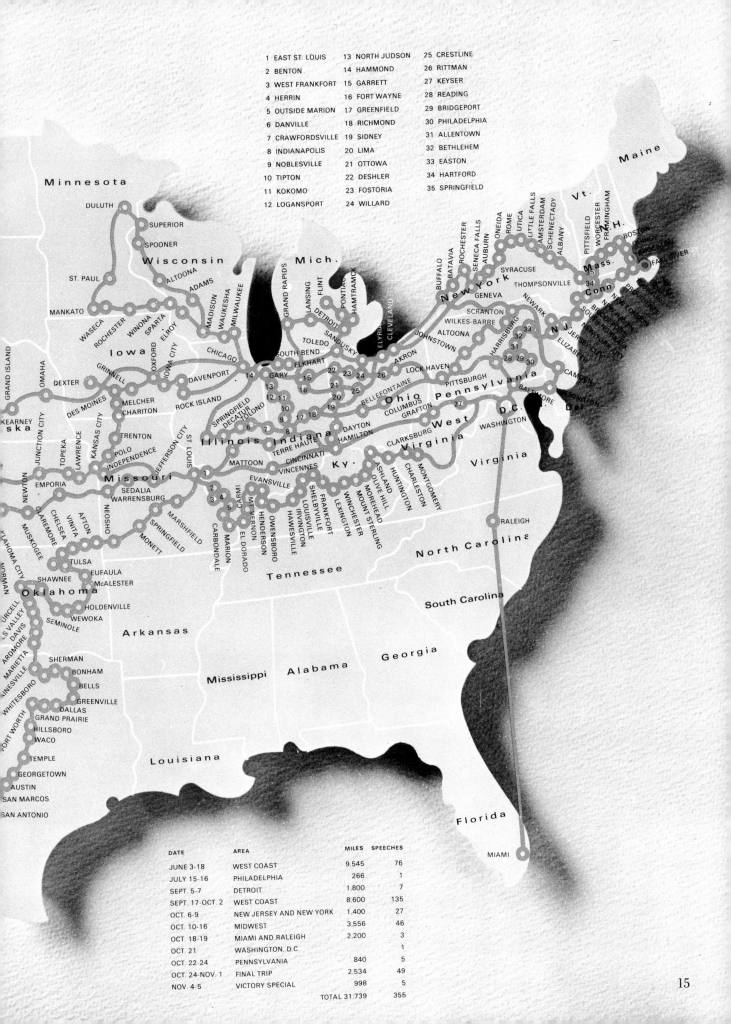

1 EAST ST. LOUIS
2 BENTON
3 WEST FRANKFORT
4 HERRIN
5 OUTSIDE MARION
6 DANVILLE
7 CRAWFORDSVILLE
8 INDIANAPOLIS
9 NOBLESVILLE
10 TIPTON
11 KOKOMO
12 LOGANSPORT

13 NORTH JUDSON
14 HAMMOND
15 GARRETT
16 FORT WAYNE
17 GREENFIELD
18 RICHMOND
19 SIDNEY
20 LIMA
21 OTTOWA
22 DESHLER
23 FOSTORIA
24 WILLARD

25 CRESTLINE
26 RITTMAN
27 KEYSER
28 READING
29 BRIDGEPORT
30 PHILADELPHIA
31 ALLENTOWN
32 BETHLEHEM
33 EASTON
34 HARTFORD
35 SPRINGFIELD

DATE	AREA	MILES	SPEECHES
JUNE 3-18	WEST COAST	9,545	76
JULY 15-16	PHILADELPHIA	266	1
SEPT. 5-7	DETROIT	1,800	7
SEPT. 17-OCT. 2	WEST COAST	8,600	135
OCT. 6-9	NEW JERSEY AND NEW YORK	1,400	27
OCT. 10-16	MIDWEST	3,556	46
OCT. 18-19	MIAMI AND RALEIGH	2,200	3
OCT. 21	WASHINGTON, D.C.		1
OCT. 22-24	PENNSYLVANIA	840	5
OCT. 24-NOV. 1	FINAL TRIP	2,534	49
NOV. 4-5	VICTORY SPECIAL	998	5
	TOTAL	31,739	355

15

RITUALS OF THE CAMPAIGN TRAIL

Performing three of the rituals that Presidential candidates must sooner or later confront, Truman hugs a child while clutching an ear of Iowa corn, accepts the gift of a student's religious painting at Boys Town, Nebraska, and chats with an Indian—Chief Robert West —dressed in full regalia in Oklahoma. Truman did such chores with unaffected ease and pleasure, his natural warmth and down-home wit coming through clearly. (He characteristically announced that while hugging babies was all right, kissing them was out: "babies can't talk and how do I know they wouldn't object?") By contrast, Truman's opponent, Dewey, was generally stiff in such circumstances, and he categorically refused to try on Indian headdresses and ten-gallon hats. It is impossible to tell, of course, how many votes Truman won—or Dewey lost—on such occasions, but the rituals of American politics gave Truman a chance to prove that he was indeed a friendly man who liked and cared for people.

❝*All over the country they call me 'Harry.' I like it. I believe when you speak to me like that you like me.*❞ —Harry S. Truman

GOOD MEN TO THE AID OF THE PARTY

Truman did not have to campaign all by himself. He gladly accepted help where he could get it, even from such dubious allies as James Roosevelt, who had been one of those in favor of "dumping" Truman before the convention, and a stuffed Democratic donkey *(below, right)*. Far more effective aid came from the Vice Presidential candidate Alben W. Barkley, shown at right with Truman, who campaigned with startling energy for a 70-year-old, making 250 speeches in 36 states. As a matter of good party politics, Walter Reuther *(top, center)*, head of the United Auto Workers, and Chicago Democratic boss Jake Arvey *(top, far right)* joined their efforts to Truman's. The nation's unions did not boost Truman enthusiastically—largely because they shared the widespread belief that he would lose. They did, however, work hard to elect pro-labor (i.e., Democratic) senators and congressmen, and Truman, as head of the ticket, got the benefit. Arvey, for his part, threw his machine into the election battle, helping the Democrats to carry Illinois.

Truman needed all the allies he could muster; as the cartoon below indicates, he faced two serious defections from the Democratic Party. The party's left wing, which disapproved of Truman's tough policy toward Russia, had split off behind former Vice President Henry A. Wallace. The right wing of conservative Southerners had also defected. Rejecting Truman's liberal civil rights views (and the party platform's strong civil rights plank), these self-styled Dixiecrats nominated South Carolina Governor Strom Thurmond for President.

BARRON IN THE ROCHESTER DEMOCRAT & CHRONICLE

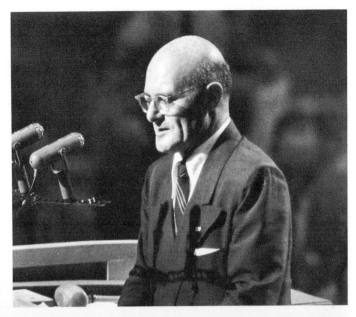

THE LAST ROUND: NEW YORK CITY

Dewey Works the East Side

Speaking before a backdrop of skyscrapers, Thomas E. Dewey winds up his campaign in his own backyard—New York. Dewey's last speeches were typical of those he gave throughout the summer and fall of 1948. They were dignified—and generally dull. As a matter of policy, his campaign was the antithesis of Truman's rousing "Give 'em hell!" performance. Dewey and his advisers, convinced that victory was certain, had settled on a strategy of not "rocking the boat." For Dewey, any sort of head-knocking confrontation with Truman was out, and he seldom responded to H.S.T.'s jibes. For the most part Dewey also refused to get down to specific cases. He was all for raising the minimum wage, for example, but he would not say by how much. Truman blistered Dewey for his vagueness. "You know where I stand," he would say. "I would like you to try to find out where the opposition stands. You'll get a lot of double talk if they ever tell you anything." Despite such attacks, and despite the clear perception on the part of some of Dewey's advisers that their candidate was boring the voters, Dewey stuck to his strategy to the end.

Truman Plays the Garden

Two powerful spotlights silhouette Truman as he speaks to a crowd of 16,000 in New York's Madison Square Garden on October 28, five nights before the election. Because the New York State Democrats had long since despaired of Truman's chances it was left to the Liberal Party—a group headed by trade unionists that votes Democratic in national elections—to pitch in and rent the Garden. In all, Truman made 13 speeches in and around New York, and in his address at the Garden made a bid for the city's large Jewish vote by saying he favored a "strong, prosperous, free and independent" Israel. Despite H.S.T.'s climactic efforts, the gloomy prognostications of the local Democrats proved true. Truman lost to Dewey in New York State, largely because 509,559 New Yorkers voted for Wallace; Dewey thus sneaked by in his home state by some 61,000 votes.

STORY OF A GARGANTUAN GOOF

While President Truman was whistle-stopping around the country, squadrons of pollsters were ringing doorbells to find out his chances of election. The samplings of public opinion assembled by the majority of pollsters told the nation, scientifically and definitively, that America's next Chief Executive would be Thomas E. Dewey. None of the three major polling organizations of that day gave Truman a chance: their estimates of the percentage of the total vote that each of the two candidates would receive are shown in the graph on the opposite page.

Lulled by the polls, newspapermen agreed that Dewey was a sure winner; a few even predicted the near-demise of the Democratic Party. Of 50 political experts questioned by a national news magazine, all 50 said that Truman could not possibly emerge the victor. They were all dead wrong.

How could the polls and the pundits have miscalculated so badly? There are many reasons. But looking back, it seems clear that the pollsters' worst mistake was to stop ringing doorbells too soon. Elmo Roper (whose forecast was the least accurate) published his last poll on September 9, almost two months before the election. His explanation: in the two previous Presidential elections, 1940 and 1944, a maximum of three per cent of the electorate had switched allegiance between September 9 and November 2. This percentage, by Roper's reasoning, was too small to alter the result he predicted for 1948. Thinking along similar lines, the Gallup poll completed its final survey in mid-October, and Crossley did the same.

The polls' paramount blunder was their failure to reflect three important events that took place in the last days of Truman's campaign. One was a sudden fall in grain prices, an economic blow that convinced many farmers they needed a man in Washington who favored price supports (i.e., a Democrat). A second key event was the collapse of Henry A. Wallace's bid for the Presidency; this change in the political climate took much of the pressure off Truman. A third factor was the cumulative effect of Truman's campaign. It is impossible to measure just how many wavering voters were swayed by Truman's hard-hitting speeches. But a post-election analysis did show that a minimum of 4.5 million voters—nearly one in every five of Truman's total of 24 million popular votes—made up their minds after mid-October. "A poll is no good," one observer said afterward, "unless it follows the voter right up to the booth."

Also contributing to the pollsters' woes was their naive assumption that the votes of people claiming to be "undecided" would be split about 50-50 between Truman and Dewey. In fact 74 per cent of the undecided cast their ballots for Truman. This was not simply a procedural mistake on the part of the poll takers; it was a basic misreading (shared by the newsmen) of the U.S. political scene. The experts failed to take into account the power and appeal of the Democratic Party, and they underestimated the lingering magnetism of Roosevelt. What happened, in essence, was that a majority of the wavering voters, who found in neither Truman nor Dewey the leadership qualities they sought, returned to voting habits built up between 1932 and 1944. That is, they voted Democratic.

In retrospect the pollsters, who have since much refined their operations, could see that they had made a number of other errors. For example, their samplings in metropolitan areas included too many middle class households, too few from lower economic and social levels. Out in the country they interviewed a disproportionate number of prosperous farmers. The professionals' failure to get down to the grass roots was demonstrated in a light-hearted "poll" conducted by a midwestern firm, the Staley Milling Company, which specializes in chicken feed. Staley offered its customers a choice of two feed sacks. One was labeled "A vote for the Republican candidate," the other, "A vote for the Democratic candidate." When the sales were tallied, Staley's results—54 per cent for the Democrats and 46 per cent for the GOP—were almost exactly on the nose.

That newspapers and magazines—and their veteran political reporters—were also wrong was due, in part, to their widespread belief in the polls. But it could also be traced to wishful thinking—some 75 per cent of all U.S. newspapers were pro-Republican—and to a conviction that the Democrats' strength had been fatally sapped by the Wallace and Dixiecrat splinter groups. Also, as the newsmen's own bitterly self-critical post mortems said over and over, they had simply not done their legwork. Arthur Krock of *The New York Times* expressed a common view: "We didn't concern ourselves, as we used to, with the facts. . . . This time, I was so sure, I made no personal investigation . . . . We have to go back to work on the old and classic lines—to the days when reporters really dug in. . . ."

On Election Day itself all this compounded error reached ludicrous proportions. Such famous columnists as the Alsop brothers, Walter Lippmann and Drew Pearson climbed out on a limb together, writing stories saying that Dewey had won. When Truman, on his way to cast his own ballot, cheerfully predicted that he would sweep the country, the reporters around him, according to his daughter Margaret, "laughed hysterically." As the evening deepened and the results poured in, it appeared that Truman was making a good fight of it. But everyone was so mesmerized by the predictions that at first only a few gloomy party workers lounged around Democratic headquarters in New York's Hotel Biltmore, while at the nearby Roosevelt crowds of gleeful Republicans celebrated. About midnight H. V. Kaltenborn, the era's leading radio pundit, gave his famous analysis: "Mr. Truman is still ahead but these are returns from a few cities. When the returns come in from the country the result will show Dewey winning overwhelmingly." The *Chicago Daily Tribune* issued an early edition whose banner headline proclaimed: "DEWEY DEFEATS TRUMAN" *(see next page).*

About the only person who believed Truman would win, it seems, was Truman himself. He was to say later that he did not believe in polls. A man could win if he simply took the truth to the people, and he felt he had done that. So he went to bed, apparently slept and was mightily annoyed when an aide awakened him after midnight with a late bulletin. He was not annoyed, however, when at 4 a.m. news came in that he led by two million votes, and it was clear that he had won. Returning to Washington in triumph, he was greeted by a sign reading, "Truman, the best pole vaulter in history." But the most accurate appraisal of Truman's victory was given by Senator Arthur Vandenberg: "There he was flat on his back. Everyone had counted him out but he came up fighting and won the battle. That's the kind of courage the American people admire."

GEORGE GALLUP

ELMO ROPER

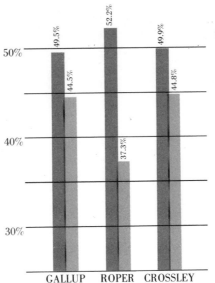

ARCHIBALD CROSSLEY

	GALLUP	ROPER	CROSSLEY
DEWEY	49.5%	52.2%	49.9%
TRUMAN	44.5%	37.3%	44.8%

A victorious Truman jubilantly holds aloft a
copy of the Chicago paper that had prematurely
proclaimed his political death. Handed the paper
when his Washington-bound "Victory Special"
paused in St. Louis, Truman exclaimed, "That's
one for the books." He was welcomed in
the capital by a shouting throng of 750,000,.

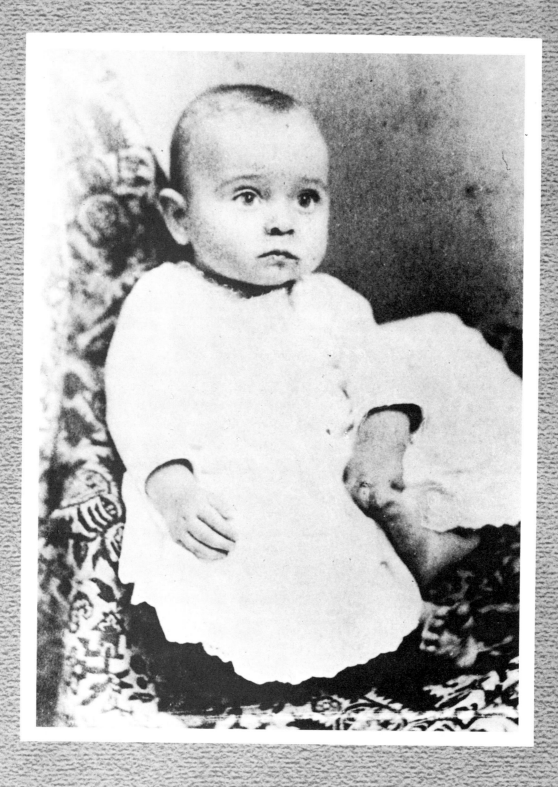

EARLY YEARS IN MISSOURI; HEROIC MOMENTS IN FRANCE

2

From the time he was born—howling loudly—on the afternoon of May 8, 1884, Harry Truman seems to have thrown himself into everything he did with the same verve and bounce he was one day to display in his conduct of the Presidency. As a boy he studied hard in school, took his piano lessons seriously, played energetically with the neighborhood gang, read voraciously. Unable to go to college after graduation from high school in 1901 because his father's finances were shaky, Truman immediately got a job as paymaster for 400 tough and profane "gandy dancers" who were laying track west of Kansas City for the Santa Fe Railway. He then worked hard at jobs in a couple of banks and finally, in 1906, took over the management of a 600-acre family farm, which he ran according to the best scientific theories of the time. As a youth, Truman's cheerful enthusiasm recommended him to just about everyone. As the foreman on the track-laying job put it with earthy Missouri vigor: "Harry's all right. He's all right from his navel out in every direction."

But his unusual energy and dedication, combined with his remarkable courage and effectiveness as a World War I officer, were the only outward signs that Harry Truman was destined for high office. In every other way, his life was that of an average Midwestern American. His family on both sides had been part of that great 19th Century movement westward that brought the Lincolns to Illinois and Mark Twain's family to eastern Missouri. Like many Missourians, they had migrated to the state from Kentucky, having moved there after generations on the East Coast. (Joseph Truman, the first American ancestor of H.S.T., had come from Nottingham, England, to New London, Connecticut, in 1666.) Like most Missourians, they were farm people. Truman's father John had been brought up on a farm and was a horse and mule trader. His mother Martha Ellen was the daughter of a successful farmer, Solomon Young, who owned the 600-acre spread H.S.T. eventually ran. Truman's people had had the courage and toughness to push westward into the Great Valley drained by the Missouri and Mississippi Rivers and, severing their ties with the East, forge for themselves a new way of life. Truman inherited this toughness along with a new, truly American culture that developed its own habits of mind and ways of speech.

Such a background was no handicap for the young Truman as he laid the foundations for the future. He picked up a remarkable knowledge of history from his reading and a knowledge of practical affairs from his various jobs, his management of a farm, his career as an officer. To his mother, the future was always clear. Asked after Truman became President if she had ever foreseen such eminence for her son, she replied, "Say, I've known that boy would amount to something from the time he was nine years old. He never did anything by halves."

Looking pensive, one-year-old Harry Truman was photographed against an ornate background of pillows.

SANTA FE TRAIL
1822 - 1872
MARKED BY THE
DAUGHTERS OF THE
AMERICAN REVOLUTION
AND THE
STATE OF MISSOURI
1909

INDEPENDENCE —

FRONTIER TOWN

Independence, Missouri, where Harry Truman grew up, is seen below in a mid-19th Century print in the days when it was a brawling frontier town. It grew up as the main eastern terminus of the Sante Fe Trail, a fact memorialized by a stone marker *(opposite)*, and long remained larger and more important than nearby Kansas City. Here rough traders and trappers congregated and shouting muleskinners assembled wagon trains bound for the West. By Truman's boyhood, it had calmed down, becoming, in the words of a school chum, "one of those places where nothing ever happened and yet everything happened."

FROM THE TRUMAN ALBUM

The 1888 photograph at right shows four-year-old Harry Truman *(standing)* and his younger brother John Vivian, both wearing dresses and high button shoes, the customary costume for small boys of that era. Vivian was born in April 1886 and a sister, Mary Jane, in 1889. The Trumans in these years lived on the farm of Solomon Young, H.S.T.'s maternal grandfather, in an agricultural area later named Grandview. They moved to Independence in 1890.

H.S.T.'s parents, John Anderson Truman and Martha Ellen Young Truman, appear prosperous and confident in a picture taken in 1881, the year they were married. The family fortunes went well for a time, but then fell off badly around the turn of the century. Truman's mother remained vigorous into her 90's, when H.S.T. was in the White House. It was after his mother's older brother, Harrison Young, that Truman was supposedly named. The family agreed to shorten his first name to Harry, but could not agree on a middle name. Some in the family wanted to call the baby Harrison Shippe Truman, taking the middle name from his paternal grandfather, but, as Truman later explained, "others . . . wanted my middle name to be Solomon, taken from my maternal grandfather. . . . No agreement could be reached and my name was recorded and stands simply as Harry S. Truman."

Harry Truman stands in the bottom row,
extreme left, of a photograph of his class at the
Noland Public School—probably taken in 1893,
his second grade year. His mother had taught
him to read before he was five, but she did not
send him to school until, at age eight, he had
been fitted with glasses. A favorite teacher,
Miss Minnie Ward, stands at upper left.

A MODEST BIRTHPLACE AND THE FAMILY FARM

The plain but sturdy farmhouse (left) was built in Grandview, Missouri, by H.S.T.'s grandfather, Solomon Young. Harry lived here between the ages of three and six, and often came over from Independence to visit during his later boyhood. It was this farm that he managed from 1906 until 1917, often doing the plowing and other heavy chores. It was taken over after World War II by his brother Vivian, shown below gazing across the barnyard. Truman's birthplace (above) still stands in Lamar, Missouri, 85 miles south of Grandview. The house was built by Truman's father in 1882, two years before H.S.T. was born. A later owner, seen standing in the yard, was Everett Earp, a relative of the famous sheriff Wyatt Earp.

SIMPLE PLEASURES OF A VANISHED TIME

The future Mrs. Harry Truman *(above, third from right)* happily buries her face in a slice of watermelon during a feast on the front lawn of her family's home in Independence. This picture of Bess Wallace and her friends was taken about 1910 by an across-the-street neighbor, Mrs. Ethel Noland (who was H.S.T.'s aunt). The picture shows *(left to right)* Bess's youngest brother Fred, Mrs. Noland's daughters Ethel and Nellie, Bess's other brothers Frank and George *(wearing a hat)*, and one of Bess's beaux of the time, Will Boger. Bess Wallace's most serious beau was always Harry Truman. In storybook style, he met her in Sunday school when he was eight and apparently never considered any other girl thereafter.

H.S.T., wearing a jaunty bow tie, and Bess Wallace *(far left)* enjoy a Missouri hayride with a group of friends during their years of courtship before World War I. Two favorite destinations for hayrides were Cave Spring, near Independence, where wagon trains had stopped for fresh water before heading west along the Santa Fe Trail, and a series of limestone ledges that had served as fortifications when Independence and its area were fought over in savage Civil War engagements between Southern-leaning guerrillas from Missouri and Northern sympathizers from neighboring Kansas.

This fine, straightforward photograph shows Bess Wallace in 1917.
Truman carried it with him when he shipped overseas in World
War I—on the back was written "to France and back—all safe"—
and it always remained his favorite portrait of his wife. The
Trumans were married after H.S.T.'s return from the War in 1919.

Shortly after he joined the National Guard in 1905, Truman was
photographed proudly wearing his uniform. When he first came
home dressed in the uniform (which was Union blue), his
grandmother, a Southern sympathizer who still remembered all too
vividly the Civil War, ordered him to get out of the house.

OFF TO FRANCE

Truman stands at ease in the field service khaki of a World War I artillery officer. He had been an enthusiastic National Guardsman during the 12 years between his enlistment and the time the U.S. entered the War, and he was elected lieutenant by the men of his unit (Guardsmen in those days chose their own junior officers). Sent to Fort Sill in Oklahoma for artillery training, he quickly proved himself an able officer—he had an uncanny knack for calculating the range of his guns—and he was promoted to captain before being sent to France as a battery commander in the 129th Field Artillery.

Captain Truman rides a rugged artillery horse at Coëtquidan, France, a French Army artillery school where he and the 129th were sent to learn the finer points of firing the French "75"— the sturdy field gun that was also used by American forces. At Coëtquidan, on July 11, 1918, he took charge of Battery D of the 129th, a unit that had won quick fame for the rough unruliness of its men. With his thick, schoolmasterish glasses, Truman looked an easy mark. But he soon proved that he was a tough soldier, well able to lead his guns through some of the War's worst fighting (pages 42-43).

IN THE THICK OF THE FIGHTING

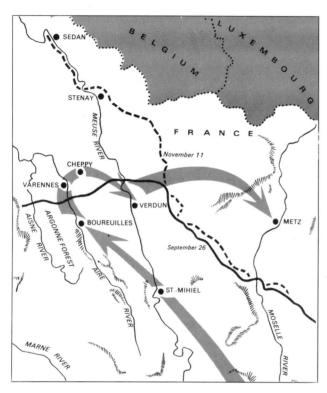

Captain Harry, as his men always called him, and his Battery D took part in the major battles fought by U.S. troops from September through November of 1918. As the arrows on the map above show, they started in a quiet sector west of the Moselle River, but were soon moved to St. Mihiel, where they took part in the all-out American advance that by September 26 was to push the German front back some 25 miles (*heavy black line*). Before the end of the St. Mihiel drive, Truman and the battery were moved to Boureuilles on the Meuse-Argonne front where, firing 3,000 rounds in four hours from their four French 75's on the morning of September 26, they helped kick off the great final offensive that by war's end would push the German lines still farther back (*dotted line*). On October 3, Battery D was transferred to the Verdun sector, where it was again in heavy fighting. As November 11 and the Armistice approached, Harry Truman and his battery were supporting American units that were preparing to attack the city of Metz.

In the last, victorious campaign of World War I, American infantrymen advance through the shell-shattered Argonne Forest, supported by a machine gun and its crew *(foreground)*. Many of the 50,510 U.S. soldiers who died in battle in the war were killed in this offensive, trying to force their way through the Argonne's tangled thickets against bitter German resistance. Backing the doughboys up, Truman's battery was in the thick of this fighting.

The men of Battery D *(right)* surround their idol Captain Harry *(circled)* at Camp Mills, New York, where they were stationed briefly after returning from France on April 20, 1919. During the 11-day voyage home, the poker-playing members of the battery set aside money from every pot and spent it to buy their commanding officer an enormous silver loving cup. Although other batteries of the 129th Field Artillery had suffered heavy casualties, Battery D, through a combination of luck and Truman's skill, had lost but one man dead and one wounded. Back in Missouri after discharge, H.S.T. renewed acquaintance with Eddie Jacobson *(left)*, whom he had known well at Fort Sill; they were soon to go into business together *(Chapter 3)*.

CAPTAIN HARRY AND HIS MEN COME HOME

Truman *(far left)* enjoys himself on summer maneuvers in the 1920s with two National Guard pals, Harry Vaughan *(center)* and John W. Snyder. H.S.T. remained in the Guard, eventually rising to the rank of colonel, and tried to get an active duty assignment when the U.S. entered World War II. At 57, he was turned down as too old. Truman was loyal to his old army friends: when he was President he made Vaughan a military aide and appointed Snyder to head several government agencies, including the Treasury.

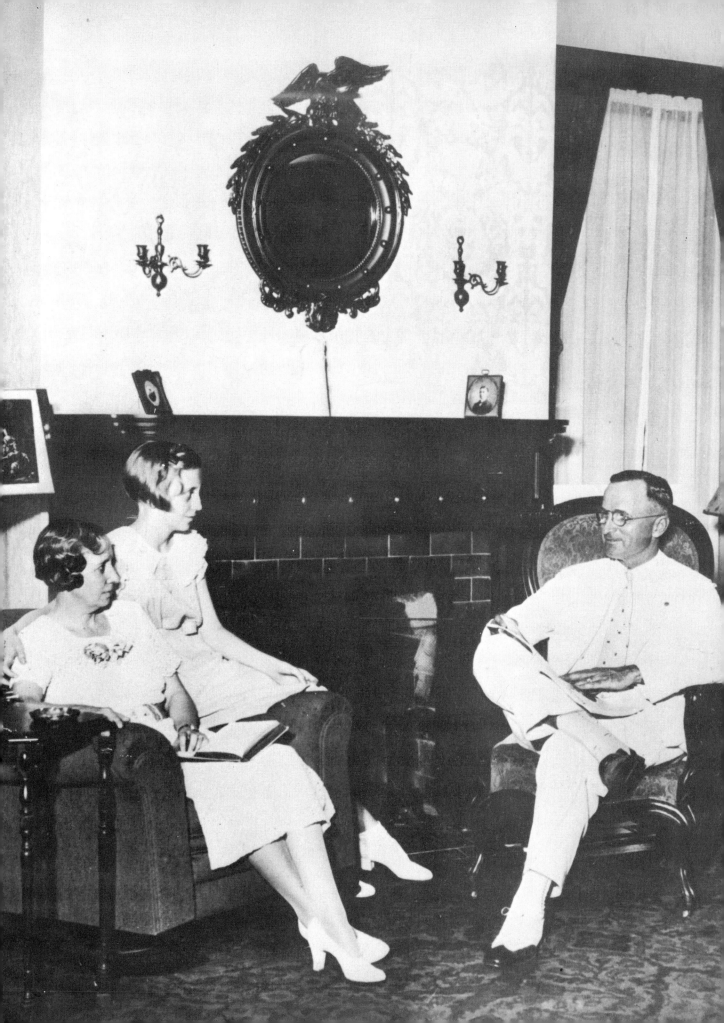

UPHILL FROM OBSCURITY

3

Two aspects of Truman's life between the end of World War I and the day he became Vice President were so lovingly, gleefully dwelt upon by his political enemies that they have all but obliterated other facts about H.S.T.'s middle years. The first is that he ran a haberdashery store that failed. The second is that he got his first political jobs with the aid of one of the 20th Century's most notorious Democratic city bosses—Kansas City's Tom Pendergast.

Both were true. Only months after leaving active duty with the Army in 1919, Truman and friend Eddie Jacobson opened a men's furnishings shop in Kansas City. It failed in 1922. In that same year Truman became the Pendergast machine's candidate for county judge and, 12 years later, in 1934, the machine's choice for U.S. Senator. For a hostile propagandist, it was a perfect image: business failure become political stooge.

But Truman's critics left out some other salient facts. The haberdashery failed during a recession caused in large part by the policies of President Warren G. Harding's Republican administration. And if Truman accepted support from Pendergast, he became famous in western Missouri, and later in the Senate, for being rigidly, precisely—almost perversely—honest in all his dealings. Boss Pendergast knew this very well, wryly calling H.S.T. "the orneriest man in Missouri."

Detractors also neglected to mention the most important fact about Truman in these years—that he made himself one of the most diligent members of the U.S. Senate. As he himself said, Truman came to the Senate in 1934 "under a cloud." Other senators assumed that he was simply a Pendergast tool. But he worked extremely hard, studying the most minute details involved in proposed legislation, putting in hard service on the Senate committees to which he was appointed and finally heading a valuable committee of his own during the early years of World War II. His fellow senators came to admire him, and he achieved full membership in that exclusive club, the inner circle of the Senate. On one occasion when Truman spoke in a debate on the floor, Republican Arthur Vandenberg, then one of the Senate's most influential members, commented, "When the Senator from Missouri makes a statement like that we can take it for the truth."

Newly elected to the Senate in 1934, Truman sits with Bess and
Margaret in the comfortable living room of their home in
Independence. Truman loved the Senate, was proud to be a member
and fought hard for reelection in 1940 after his first term was up.

THE FAMOUS, ILL-FATED HABERDASHERY

A jaunty Truman (*far left*) leans against a counter in the menswear shop he helped found in 1919 at 104 West 12th Street, Kansas City— which became a hangout for members of his old artillery battery like those seen in the background. Truman and his partner Jacobson, seen above in another shop he ran much later, had high hopes for their venture since both had proved their business acumen while running a successful PX during wartime training at Fort Sill, Oklahoma. The shop did well at first, but in 1922 an agricultural depression—which Truman was later to blame on Eastern financiers and the Republicans in Congress—struck the Midwest. With their customers going broke, Truman and Jacobson did too. Jacobson, who "stayed in the shirt business," died in 1955.

POLITICS WITH PENDERGAST

Truman always remained friends with the jowly man who gave him his start in politics, Thomas J. Pendergast (shown below conferring with H.S.T. at the 1936 Democratic Convention). Pendergast was a king among old-fashioned political bosses; the bottom picture at right shows him lording it with fellow Democratic satraps including James A. Farley *(far right)*. The Pendergast machine was as corrupt as any; a typical practice in its wards was "voting ghosts"—stuffing ballot boxes with the votes of people who had died, or never existed. But Pendergast never leaned on Truman to do anything dishonest; as H.S.T. said later, "He knew I wouldn't do it if he had asked me."

As presiding judge of Jackson County in the late 1920s and early 1930s, Truman experiments with a device for simultaneously signing five checks. Truman was not a judge in the usual sense of presiding at trials. Instead his job was to oversee the county roads, the courthouse and other public works, negotiate contracts for repairs and upkeep and pay the county's bills. He was highly successful at the job. Before he left it to become a Senator he had refurbished the Independence courthouse (with a statue of his idol, President Andrew Jackson, in front), had all of the roads improved and managed the county's finances so well that they showed a handsome surplus.

MR. TRUMAN GOES TO WASHINGTON

The Trumans admire their 1934 Chrysler *(left)* shortly before leaving for Washington and H.S.T.'s new job as Senator from Missouri. Truman worked hardest as a member of the Interstate Commerce Committee on an investigation of the financial condition of the nation's railroads, assiduously plowing through piles of documents in his office *(below)*. In one of his best-remembered Senate speeches, he said that train robber Jesse James was a piker compared to some railroad executives who were milking their own roads of millions.

H.S.T. tends the toaster while Bess makes breakfast in the small kitchen of their Washington apartment. The Trumans were forced to live modestly during the Senate years; the yearly Senate salary was then only $10,000, and Truman, unlike many senators then and now, had no other source of income. Home was a rather cramped four rooms off Connecticut Avenue that rented for $120 a month; among their few extravagances was a piano for Margaret. Truman enjoyed himself immensely nonetheless. As he said later, "The Senate, that's just my speed and my style."

SOLID SUCCESS IN THE SENATE

The "Truman Committee" of the Senate was formed in 1941 at H.S.T.'s suggestion. Its purpose is explained by its official title: Special Committee to Investigate the National Defense Program. And investigate it did, looking hard at every aspect of the nation's mighty effort to arm against German and Japanese aggression.

The inspiration for the committee came in early 1941 when several constituents informed Truman that there were scandalous waste and inefficiency in the construction of Fort Leonard Wood near Waynesville, Missouri. Truman went and looked for himself and found the charges all too true. Then he drove some 30,000 miles through the nation looking into camps, plants and mills. What he saw made his blood boil. Not only were there graft and extravagance, but also clear evidence that defense contracts were going almost exclusively to big companies while smaller firms were being denied contracts and forced to the wall. Truman reported his observations to the Senate, which responded by authorizing a committee and, for a starter, $15,000 in operating expenses. The original seven members of the committee were all relatively young, except for wise old Tom Connally of Texas, and they set to work with enthusiasm, holding many hearings in Washington and also traveling around the country to visit aircraft plants, training camps, shipyards and other installations. Back in Washington, the committee often met in a small room behind Truman's Senate office called "the doghouse" and there prepared its reports. The Senators found incredible mismanagement. A Quartermaster Corps decision to rent construction equipment rather than buy it, for example, cost the treasury a needless $13 million. They also found bungling on a tragic scale: engines that did not fit the aircraft they were designed for; a bomber whose wings were too small for stable flight. When they uncovered such waste and ineptitude, Truman and his committee came down hard. They forced reforms on the Army, the Navy, many manufacturers and the War Production Board. In the process they saved the taxpayers an estimated $15 billion—and doubtless saved many lives as well.

Truman inspects the engine of an A-20A Douglas medium bomber in 1942 with Carl Cover, Douglas' chief test pilot. H.S.T. personally visited hundreds of war plants, inquiring into all the equipment they produced.

Members of the Truman Committee gather for a meeting in the tiny office called the "doghouse." Left to right are committee attorney Hugh Fulton and Senators Tom Connally, Joseph Ball, H.S.T., Harley Kilgore and Owen Brewster.

Nobody was more surprised than Truman to discover at the Democratic National Convention in 1944 that he was a front runner for the Vice Presidential nomination. He did not seek the job and had even agreed to support the candidacy of Governor James F. Byrnes of South Carolina. Meanwhile, most people assumed that Vice President Henry A. Wallace still had Roosevelt's support and was the most likely nominee. But the professional politicians and the leaders of labor had been getting together. The politicians did not like Wallace, who was a liability in the South, where he was considered a dangerous radical. Southerner Byrnes, it turned out, was too conservative for labor. The top Democrats and union heads then settled on Truman and their choice was approved by F.D.R. Truman at first refused to believe that Roosevelt wanted him, but was convinced when Democratic Committee Chairman Robert Hannegan picked up a phone, called F.D.R. and got a ringing confirmation.

Among the politicians who helped pick Truman for the Vice Presidency were the two old pros seen at left, Mayor Ed Kelly of Chicago *(wearing glasses)* and Frank Hague of New Jersey. Labor leaders such as Philip Murray *(below, left)* and Sidney Hillman of the CIO, seen at a Convention conference, also favored H.S.T. as their second choice after Henry Wallace. In fact, it was Hillman who first told Truman that, whether he wanted to be or not, he was an active candidate. Boss Hague spoke for the big city Democratic organizations: "If President Roosevelt is for Truman, I'm for him."

TRUMAN'S CONVENTION VICTORY

Democratic Party Chairman Samuel Jackson lifts Vice Presidential nominee Truman's arm high in triumph on the evening of July 21, 1944. On a second ballot, seldom needed for a Vice Presidential nomination, H.S.T. had narrowly beaten Henry Wallace.

Tenacious, vocal supporters of Wallace for Vice President *(left)*, mill around the convention hall in Chicago trying to sustain the boom for their candidate *(top, left)*. They almost managed to take the convention by storm before the Truman forces, carefully lined up by Hannegan, could bring their power to bear. The candidacy of James F. Byrnes *(top, right)* had been deflated when it became clear that neither labor nor Roosevelt favored his nomination.

WINNING CAMPAIGN WITH F.D.R.

Roosevelt and Truman ride in the rain *(right)* from Washington's Union Station to the White House on November 10, 1944, after winning the election. Truman had campaigned hard after getting the Vice Presidential nomination, traveling around the country in an old Pullman car called the *Henry Stanley* and making speeches from the back platform, much as he was to do in 1948. Republican newspapers, afraid to attack Roosevelt because he was still the nation's war leader, concentrated their fire on Truman. Sample charges: onetime membership in the Ku Klux Klan and addiction to gambling. Truman denounced such allegations as lies, but they did not really worry him. What concerned him most—"it scares the hell out of me," he told a friend—was the thought that F.D.R. might not survive the next four years and that the Presidency would be thrust on him.

In shirtsleeves, Truman and Roosevelt meet for lunch at a table on the White House lawn on August 18, 1944—after the Democratic Convention but before their campaign got under way. Sitting in the shade of an immense magnolia tree planted a hundred years before by President Andrew Jackson, the two men had a lively, friendly talk. Unfortunately, it was one of the few talks Truman ever had with Roosevelt. Truman was on the campaign trail until the election in November; after that F.D.R. was so busy he seldom had a chance to see his new Vice President.

A WEARY ROOSEVELT'S LAST INAUGURAL

President Roosevelt, flanked by a Secret Service man, his son James (then a Marine colonel) and a somber Truman, delivers his fourth inaugural address from the porch of the White House. Almost 63 years old, F.D.R. looked grey and tired, but insisted on standing coatless in a cold January wind. His speech was the shortest of his inaugural addresses: 5 minutes, 551 words. He left to attend the Yalta meeting with Churchill and Stalin soon after, returning so exhausted that he shortly left Washington again for Warm Springs, Georgia—where he died.

Truman leans over to shake hands and talk with Mrs. Eleanor Roosevelt at a post-election banquet. Mrs. Roosevelt was already aware that F.D.R.'s health was failing, but so as not to alarm either friends or the public, she never gave any outward sign of concern.

THE DEATH OF ROOSEVELT
AND A LEGACY
OF CRISES FOR TRUMAN

4

On the evening of the grim day in 1945 that Franklin D. Roosevelt died, Harry Truman repeated the simple oath of office and became President of the United States. It was about the last simple thing Truman would be called upon to do for the next seven and three-quarter years. Seldom has a U.S. President taken office in a period of greater crisis. In April 1945, the war in Europe was drawing to its grim climax and the war against Japan seemed to promise at least another year of appalling carnage. Europe lay shattered and threatened by wholesale starvation. Russia, still an ally, was already giving signs of postwar intransigence as it brazenly (and in defiance of its agreements) installed Communist governments in the reconquered nations of Eastern Europe. At home, the nation heaved with a gigantic restlessness, impatient under wartime restrictions, yet filled with foreboding that the War's end and reconversion to a peacetime economy would bring on a catastrophic depression.

These were but a few of the problems that Truman—lacking even perfunctory briefings on current plans and policies by his dead predecessor, advised by a Cabinet whose members he did not really know—immediately confronted. And they were but the first of a seemingly unending string of crises in both foreign and domestic affairs that followed in the first months, and years, of his Presidency and continued to the last.

As he shouldered the gigantic burdens of his new office, Truman was an unknown quantity to the nation—despite his brilliant wartime work on the "Truman Committee" in the Senate. He was also unknown to such paramount world leaders as Winston Churchill, who had profound doubts that this new, untried man would prove capable of dealing with the remaining problems of the War and the ter-

Playing his accordion in tribute to the fallen President, Navy, musician Graham Jackson weeps as Franklin D. Roosevelt's coffin leaves Warm Springs, Georgia, where the President died. Chief Petty Officer Jackson, who had often entertained Roosevelt, had been summoned to Warm Springs to cheer the vacationing F.D.R.

rifyingly complex challenges of the peace to follow. Truman quickly surprised everyone by the vigor he showed in meeting crisis after crisis. If he was new to the office, he understood its great basic requirement—decisiveness. Not all of his decisions were wise, especially during his first months as President, and some boomeranged badly. Many were unpopular: first and last, he managed to alienate, if in many cases only temporarily, virtually every segment of United States and world opinion. He both sharpened Russia's suspicions and caused Britain severe financial embarrassment by ordering what he later realized to have been an intemperately abrupt halt to the Lend-Lease Program. He was berated at War's end for not demobilizing America's fighting forces more swiftly. Later, when Russia's aggressive tendencies became more obvious, he was criticized for having let U.S. military might shrink to a point of weakness that openly invited Russian aggression. He was roundly denounced by conservatives for being "soft on Communism," especially after it was discovered that some Soviet agents had been operating successfully in the U.S. Meanwhile he had to withstand constant sniping from liberals who blamed his so-called "get tough" policy toward Russian expansionism for Russia's increasingly hostile stance.

"... you're crazy as hell. I am going to protect the public."

Many of Truman's problems had one awesome characteristic in common: they offered no wholly correct solution. Again and again, Truman faced the dilemma of choosing the lesser of two evils. In his handling of a rash of strikes that broke out as the War was coming to a close, these quandaries are glaringly apparent. Truman was by nature and conviction—dating back to his own days on the farm—in favor of the workingman. As he said over and over, the basis of his political philosophy was that the government of the U.S. should further the interests of the average citizen, not the "big interests." He knew that miners worked their backbreaking shifts in perilous conditions for too little money; he saw that steelworkers and railroadmen should have greater rewards for their vital labors. However, after John L. Lewis, the tough, passionate boss of the United Mine Workers, closed the nation's mines in 1946, when both the U.S. and war-ravaged Europe were perilously low on coal, Truman acted swiftly—even brutally—to take over the mines and force the miners back to work. He responded the same way when strikes crippled the railroads and the steel industry. In Truman's view, he had to keep the country's economy moving, especially during the desperate, crowded days that came with the ending of the War. "If you think I'm going to sit here and let you tie up this country," he told the railroad union leaders, "you're crazy as hell. I am going to protect the public. . . ." These actions, of course, earned Truman deep and long-lasting enmity among the very forces of labor whose cause he instinctively espoused.

However tortuous the dilemmas, however tough the decisions, Truman did decide. He acted. He led. He got frustratingly little of the domestic legislation he considered vital for the nation's welfare, but he never let up in his pressure for action. After a brief "honeymoon" with Congress, Truman faced generally sullen Congresses ruled either by conservative Republicans or by a coalition of Republicans and equally conservative Southern Democrats. He sent request after request to Capitol Hill for a wide variety of bills—public housing, fair employment practices, improved social security, more TVA-style public power projects—only to see them die there, or be legislated to death in watered-down, ineffective laws.

Fortunately for Truman, the nation and the world, the Congress was far more cooperative when it came to foreign affairs. Onetime isolationist Senator Arthur Vandenberg performed wonders in keeping foreign policy bi-partisan, particularly in the crucial area of foreign aid. And it was in foreign affairs that Truman faced, acted on and in many cases overcame a staggering number of crises of the first magnitude, in the process guiding America to its inevitable (if painful) postwar position as the great leader of the free world.

Altogether, Truman's record in foreign policy was remarkable. As his last Secretary of State, Dean Acheson, later put it, "A Truman policy is as easily recognized as Chippendale furniture and has stood the test of years as well. When the Truman government found its footing in foreign affairs, its policies showed a sweep, a breadth of concentration and boldness of action which were new in this country's history. All of them were dangerous. All required rare capacity to decide and act. All of them were decided rightly and vigorously followed through."

"A Truman policy is as easily recognized as Chippendale furniture. . ."

Only a few weeks after taking office, Truman was faced by one of the most momentous decisions any man ever had to make—the decision to drop the atom bomb. But even before that he had had to survive a number of ordeals. He met threats from ambitious leaders he called "little Caesars"—De Gaulle and Tito— who arose as the war in Europe came to an end, helped nurse the United Nations into existence, and met with Churchill and Stalin at Potsdam in an attempt to map a peaceful course for the postwar world. Soon afterward he was awash in a mounting tide of foreign crises—civil war in China, a Russian threat to the Middle East, the Soviet blockade of Berlin. As the overall threat of Russian expansionism became more and more evident, Truman pushed through epochal programs that effectively blunted Soviet pressure and saved much of Europe from becoming Communist. Finally, when the then still monolithic Communist bloc decided to test American resolve by turning the Cold War hot in Korea, Truman once again responded decisively (Chapter 6).

Despite bold and successful policies abroad, the Republican press and Truman's enemies in Congress seldom let up in their criticisms, even after Truman had proved by winning re-election in 1948 that he had the people on his side (Chapter 1). Few Presidents have been so flayed and—except for a few outbursts of temper —few have appeared so unconcerned. To most criticisms, Truman responded fatalistically. As he said when two would-be assassins tried to gun him down: "A President has to expect those things." Through all the crises and criticisms he faced, he remained himself, Harry Truman, his bouncy, perky exterior concealing the fact that he was a very courageous and very serious President doing his level best to lead the nation and the world to a better, less perilous future.

FAREWELL TO A HERO-LEADER

The traditional horse-drawn caisson carries
Franklin D. Roosevelt's flag-draped coffin
through the streets of Washington as mourners,
many weeping openly, line the route. The
cortege took the late President's body, which
Mrs. Roosevelt had brought north from Warm
Springs, from the Washington station to the
White House for a simple funeral.

A SWIFT AND SOLEMN SWEARING IN

Vice President Truman had just finished presiding over a lazy session of the Senate and was about to have a nip of bourbon with House Speaker Sam Rayburn when he got word that the White House had called. The message: call back. Truman talked to Roosevelt's press secretary, Steven Early. "Please come right over," Early said in an odd, strangled voice.

Watching Truman as he listened, Rayburn saw his face turn ashen and heard him mutter, "Holy General Jackson." Truman left the Speaker's office, ran to his car and sped to the White House. There he was met by Mrs. Roosevelt, who put her arm on his shoulder and said, "Harry, the President is dead." "Is there anything I can do for you?" Truman asked, blinking back tears. "Is there anything *we* can do for *you?*" she replied. "For you are the one in trouble now."

In this fashion Harry Truman discovered that he had become President of the United States. He quickly called Bess and Margaret and summoned Chief Justice Harlan Stone to swear him in. At precisely 7:09, one minute short of two hours after his telephone conversation with Early, Truman took the oath of office.

Chief Justice Stone administers the oath of office to Harry S. Truman in the White House Cabinet Room as members of the Cabinet, Congressional leaders, Bess and Margaret look on. The somber expressions on the faces of those present reflect not only the importance of the occasion, but also the fact that everyone was fighting tears of grief for Roosevelt's death. As Truman recalled later, "everyone was crying. . . . None of us could believe that F.D.R. was gone." After the swearing in, official photographs were taken, including a formal portrait of the new First Family *(right)*. Then Truman, with the swift decisiveness he was to display so often as President, called a meeting of the Cabinet and assured its members that he would vigorously pursue Roosevelt's foreign and domestic policies. Truman also gave his first Presidential order: the San Francisco conference that was to draft the U.N. Charter would meet as scheduled. Then he went home to his old $120 a month apartment on Connecticut Avenue and ate a ham sandwich provided by a neighbor.

❝*Boys, if you ever pray, pray for me now. I don't know whether you fellows ever had a load of hay fall on you, but when they told me yesterday what had happened [to Roosevelt], I felt like the moon, the stars and all the planets had fallen on me.***❞** — Harry S. Truman to reporters, April 13, 1945

A GRIEF-STRICKEN, WORRIED CHURCHILL

Britain's great Prime Minister bites his lip in grief outside London's St. Paul's Cathedral after a memorial service for Roosevelt. Like all Englishmen, Churchill mourned the President's death as the loss of a friend. He also shared with many of his countrymen—and a great many Americans as well—a profound concern about Truman's ability to carry the War to its conclusion and then deal with the problems of peace. Who was this man Truman? Churchill knew little more than most U.S. citizens about H.S.T. He *did* know that a U.S. Vice President was largely excluded from the councils and decisions of the Presidency. As Churchill wrote later, "the Vice President of the United States steps at a bound from a position where he has little information and less power into supreme authority. How could Mr. Truman know and weigh the issues at stake in this climax of the War?" Churchill later came to admire Truman as a "fearless man, capable of taking the greatest decisions." But at the moment of Roosevelt's death, the man from Missouri appeared to Churchill as a poor substitute for F.D.R.

ASSURANCE FROM AN OLD NEWSMAN

Two veteran Missouri journalists wrote articles soon after Truman became President assuring the American people that H.S.T. was quite capable of handling the job. One was cigar-chomping Roy Roberts (*right*), managing editor of the Kansas City *Star;* the other was Charles G. Ross, a boyhood friend of Truman's and the Washington correspondent of the St. Louis *Post-Dispatch (opposite).* Roberts had been a leading crusader against the Pendergast machine, but he knew that although Truman had benefited politically from the machine, he was an honest and capable man. To Roberts, Truman was the epitome of the "average man"—a quality he felt might prove Truman's "greatest asset," for it would enable him to understand the people's needs. On a couple of issues Roberts' crystal ball was clouded. He predicted that H.S.T. would get along with Congress well; this unhappily proved untrue. He also said that Truman's innate Missouri conservatism would lead him to temper Roosevelt's liberal programs. In fact, Truman was more outspoken on such issues as civil rights than F.D.R. ever was.

GOOD MARKS FROM AN IMPORTANT BRITON

Britain's Foreign Secretary Anthony Eden had paused in Washington on his way to the U.N. Charter meeting in San Francisco when news came of Roosevelt's death. He stayed in the capital to attend the funeral and also to meet the new President, making a courtesy call on Truman on the morning of April 16—Truman's fourth day in office. The meeting was friendly, and Eden's first view of H.S.T. was generally favorable— as he hastened to inform Churchill by cable: "My impression from the interview is that the new President is honest and friendly. He is conscious of but not over-whelmed by his new responsibilities. His references to you could not have been warmer. I believe we shall have in him a loyal collaborator. . . ." Years later in his memoirs Eden was more positive: "I liked him immediately. Greatness was thrust upon Truman, but he never let his knowledge of this daunt his courage or his power of decision." Churchill was doubtless cheered by Eden's report, and as a historian, drew comfort from intelligence he received that Truman had a remarkable and detailed knowledge of history.

A BOYHOOD FRIEND TALKS OF TRUMAN

Charlie Ross, a classmate of Truman's who served as Presidential Press Secretary from 1945 until his death in 1950, wrote a perceptive "personal impression" of H.S.T. for his St. Louis paper two days after the swearing in. After recalling H.S.T.'s early political battles, Ross went on to assess the new Chief Executive. "Will Truman measure up? A firm answer cannot yet be given. But this can safely be said: Harry Truman has a lot of stuff—more stuff, I think, than he has generally been credited with. . . . He is no nonentity. . . . He may not have the makings of a great President, but he certainly has the makings of a good President." Ross, one of the many Missourians Truman appointed to his staff, proved an able spokesman for the President. He should, according to a 44-year-old prediction, have been President himself. On high school graduation day in 1901 an English teacher everybody called Miss Tillie gave Charlie a kiss because he had been her best scholar (Truman was next best). Asked why she had done it, Miss Tillie said jokingly, "I hope yet to kiss a President of the United States."

FRAMING THE CHARTER
OF THE UNITED NATIONS

The United Nations was created in the spring of 1945 in San Francisco, where 800 delegates from 46 nations met to work out a charter for the new international body. It was not easy going; two months passed between the first meeting on April 25 and the speech Truman gave (*right*) to the last session on June 25. Much of the trouble and delay could be traced to the intransigence of the Soviet Union's chief representative, Vyacheslav M. Molotov. Truman became so worried that the Russians would scuttle the whole proceeding that he sent Harry Hopkins, Roosevelt's trusted right-hand man, to Moscow to reason with Stalin. The stratagem worked, for Stalin instructed Molotov to soften his objections. The members of the U.S. delegation, whose signatures appear on the page of the Charter shown below, included Secretary of State Edward Stettinius, who is seated at the table next to Truman in the picture at right, and Senators Tom Connally, Arthur Vandenberg and Harold Stassen. Alger Hiss—seated at far right under the flags—who was to become the center of a storm of controversy (*pages 90-91*), was the U.S. mission's top executive officer.

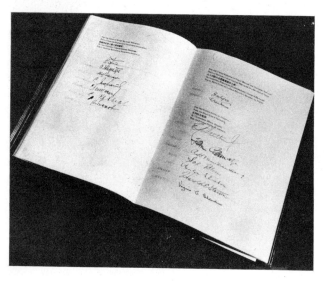

Senator Arthur Vandenberg pauses during a speech he gave at the San Francisco Conference urging the right of regional groups, such as the Americas, to spring to their own defense without U.N. sanction if attacked. Vandenberg, a former isolationist, was perhaps the most important member of the U.S. mission to the Charter meetings since his great influence in the Senate virtually guaranteed that the body would ratify U.S. membership in the U.N. Vandenberg's conversion to internationalism allayed fears that the Senate would repeat the error it made in 1919 when, led by Henry Cabot Lodge Sr., it scuttled the League of Nations by refusing to let the U.S. join that earlier attempt at international cooperation. The Senate vote, taken in July 1945, was 89 to 2 in favor of the U.N. The U.S. was the first nation to ratify.

Truman shares a joke with Eleanor Roosevelt during a banquet in honor of her 75th birthday. The year the U.N. Charter was signed, Truman appointed Mrs. Roosevelt to America's U.N. delegation, a post she held for six years. Mrs. Roosevelt was an admirer of H.S.T., as he was of her. In her autobiography she wrote that Truman "had a remarkable understanding of the office and duties of the President. I felt," she continued, "that he had had to make more than his share of big decisions . . . and that he made few mistakes in times of crisis."

Massed G.I.'s entirely cover the wide afterdecks
of the *Queen Elizabeth* as the world's
largest liner steams into New York Harbor on
June 29, 1945. The Queen carried some 14,000
soldiers per trip as the U.S. rushed its forces
home from Europe after V.E. Day. Truman was
later to be criticized for bringing too
many troops back to the U.S. too soon.

THE BIG THREE AT POTSDAM

Dramatic changes in leadership are reflected in the two official photographs *(left)* taken at Potsdam in July 1945. In the top picture the presence of Truman was a visual surprise to those used to seeing F.D.R., who had sat for so many earlier allied-conference pictures with Churchill and Stalin. The presence of Clement Attlee in the bottom row was an even more surprising change. In the middle of the Potsdam meetings, Britain held a general election. Churchill's Conservative Party lost to Attlee's Labour Party. Attlee succeeded Churchill in the office of Prime Minister and represented Britain at the last Potsdam talks.

The War against Germany finally concluded, both Truman and Churchill decided that a meeting with Stalin was in order. Many problems concerning the future of the defeated Reich remained to be solved; in addition, the President and the Prime Minister were both disturbed by Moscow's refusal to set up a freely elected and independent government in Poland, as the Soviets had agreed to do at the 1945 Yalta Conference. It appeared that Stalin was going to shroud Eastern Europe behind what Churchill was already privately calling "an iron curtain." Stalin agreed to a meeting and chose the Berlin suburb of Potsdam as a site.

During the first few sessions of the conference, Truman found Stalin sympathetic and said he was "as near like Tom Pendergast as any man I know." Churchill, he felt, was tiresomely longwinded. But as meeting followed meeting with only the most minuscule progress being made, Truman's enthusiasm for the Soviet leader waned. In later years, he would be much criticized for allowing the Soviets to impose on the other Allies "temporary" four-power agreements that, in effect, became the permanent outline of a divided modern Germany; he was also faulted for blandly accepting broad Russian interpretations of such words as "democratic" and "justice" when it came to Soviet promises of "free elections" in such countries as Poland. But he was a novice President who had inherited the wartime optimism of F.D.R. about the Soviet ally. In addition, he was handicapped by the fact that his advisers, and U.S. policy-makers in general, were then woefully ignorant about Russian affairs.

The most momentous thing that happened to Truman at Potsdam had nothing to do with the basic agenda of the Big Three meetings. On July 16, the day before the first session, Truman got word that an atom bomb had been successfully exploded at Alamogordo, New Mexico. He immediately told Churchill and later Stalin. Both unhesitatingly urged Truman to use the new weapon against Japan *(pages 80-81).*

THE FRIGHTFUL BLASTS THAT ENDED THE WAR

The decision to drop the atomic bomb on Japan, as Truman saw it at the time, was inevitable. He had, he felt, little choice. The Japanese had given no indication that they would surrender; rather, they seemed intent on fighting to the last man, as their 85,000-man garrison on Okinawa was then doing. Truman's military chiefs estimated that an invasion of the Japanese home islands would cost between 500,000 and a million casualties, including 175,000 dead—twice as many Americans as had been killed in the European theater. There was no telling how many million Japanese soldiers and civilians would die.

Before giving the order to drop the bomb, Truman issued an ultimatum calling on Japan to surrender. The official answer from that nation's warlords: "absurd." Some historians have since found evidence that Japan was closer to signing a surrender than its official answer indicated. They have also found some indication that Truman was aware of this and therefore should not have ordered the bomb dropped. Truman always stoutly denied these allegations, saying, "I did not hesitate to order the use of the bomb. . . . I wanted to save a half million boys on our side and as many on the other side." Churchill concurred: "There never was a moment's discussion as to whether the atomic bomb should be used or not. To avert a vast, indefinite butchery, to bring the War to an end . . . seemed after all our toils and perils, a miracle of deliverance."

Hiroshima lies in ruins with only a few walls standing *(below)* after the first atom bomb struck the city at 9:15 a.m. on August 6 (Japanese time), 1945. The bomb, small by later standards, contained an explosive force equal to 20,000 tons of TNT. It burst 150 feet above Hiroshima's Military Park, killing or injuring 75,000 people. Three days later a second bomb was dropped on Nagasaki; its mushroom cloud, erupting out of a dark column of fire, is shown at left. In Nagasaki 35,000 people died or were injured.

THE FRUITLESS STRUGGLE FOR CHINA

No problem that faced Truman was more vexed and—as it turned out—insoluble than that of China. When World War II ended, China was, as Truman quickly realized, "only a geographical expression." Chiang Kai-shek's nationalist government held sway only in the southwest corner of the gigantic country. Mao Tse-tung's Communists controlled the North, and the Russians occupied Manchuria. The rest of China was in the hands of the Japanese Army. The Japanese eventually departed, but this only left the field open for the Nationalists and the Communists to start battling each other. To try to heal this breach, Truman sent General George C. Marshall to China as mediator. The general quickly arranged a cease fire, signed on January 13, 1946, by Communist leader Chou En-lai (*below, seated*) as Nationalist General Chang Chon and Marshall watched. He even persuaded the Nationalists and the Communists to form a coalition government. But hawks in both camps soon precipitated new fighting. The U.S. government did what it could to save Chiang, sending some two billion dollars in aid. It did little good, especially when corrupt Nationalist generals sold their U.S.-supplied arms to the Reds; in 1949 Chiang's government fled to Taiwan. Truman is still castigated by some for "losing China" to the Communists, but it seems clear he could have "saved" China only by invading it with a large U.S. army.

A HELPING HAND FOR A FLEDGLING ISRAEL

From the time he took office, Truman favored the establishment of the state of Israel. But his advocacy involved him in a thicket of controversy. On the one hand he had to wage a long diplomatic battle with the British who controlled Palestine and did not want a Jewish nation established there. On the other hand, Truman had to withstand the pressure exerted on him by extreme U.S. Zionists, who badgered him unmercifully to move faster toward creating Israel.

British objections to Israel were practical. They foresaw—correctly—that carving a Jewish homeland from an area the Arabs considered theirs would lead to warfare. This in turn would jeopardize Western access to the Middle East's enormous and vital supplies of oil. Truman's approach was humanitarian. He felt that after the horrors European Jews had suffered at the hands of the Nazis, the survivors ought to be given a sanctuary where they could rebuild their lives. After a great deal of wrangling, the government of Prime Minister Attlee gave way, declaring that the British mandate over Palestine would end on May 14, 1948. This opened the way for the great Jewish leader, Dr. Chaim Weizmann, to declare that the state of Israel existed. To back him up, Truman quickly extended official U.S. recognition to the new Israeli government. Shortly thereafter Dr. Weizmann called on Truman (*below*) to offer his and his nation's thanks.

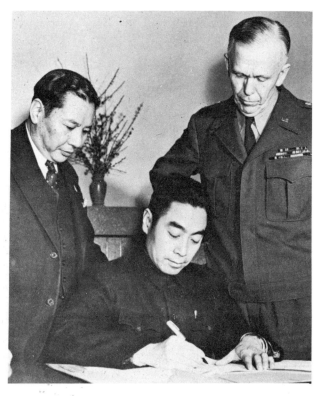

ARMS AND AID
TO SHORE UP EUROPE

Always paramount among Truman's concerns was the threat posed by Russian expansionism. Early in 1947 it seemed clear that the Soviets were going to try to muscle their way into Iran and Turkey and to inspire a Communist takeover in Greece. Truman moved forcefully, ordering the U.S. Navy into the Eastern Mediterranean to warn Stalin that Iran and Turkey were off limits, and then sending aid to Greece that helped stave off its Communist guerrillas. In making these moves, Truman clearly indicated that henceforth it would be U.S. policy to resist aggression wherever it occurred. This policy was quickly dubbed the Truman Doctrine. It was evident, however, that more positive moves were called for. Above all, Europe's shattered economy had to be shored up. Truman, with Secretary of State Marshall and his assistant, Dean Acheson, conceived the Marshall Plan—a massive, historic and successful aid program that, beginning in 1948, put Europe back on its feet. Even this, Truman felt, was not enough. Europe needed a military shield against possible Russian attack. From that conviction emerged NATO—the North Atlantic Treaty Organization—designed to help Europe re-arm and ultimately to unify its fighting forces with those of the U.S. In the photograph below Secretary of State Acheson, watched by Truman and Vice President Barkley, signs the NATO pact on behalf of the U.S. on April 4, 1949.

BOLD AIRLIFT FOR
BLOCKADED BERLIN

An Air Force C-54 Skymaster cargo plane wings into Berlin's Tempelhof airfield (below), flying over the rubble of the war-shattered city during the great Berlin Airlift of 1948-1949. The airlift, which performed the incredible task of providing food and fuel for 2,400,000 Berliners for almost a year, was Truman's forceful but measured response to Russia's most provocative expansionist move in Europe up to that time—the blockade of the city, part of which is an island of Western-style democracy surrounded by Communist East Germany. The blockade began in earnest on June 24, 1948, when the Soviet Army sealed off all access to Berlin by rail or highway from the West, leaving the city isolated 110 miles behind the Iron Curtain. Truman saw this as a concerted attempt to force the U.S., Britain and France out of their occupation zones in the divided city. On June 25 he announced to his Cabinet that "We are going to stay. Period!" And on the 26th he ordered all U. S. Air Force cargo planes in Europe to start regular runs to Berlin. By mid-July 132 aircraft were making two trips a day each, carrying a total of 2,500 tons of goods daily. This flow was steadily expanded with British help until on April 16 of the next year a record 12,941 tons was flown over the Russian roadblocks. The Soviet leaders eventually saw that they were not going to starve the Allies out of Berlin and called off their blockade on May 12, 1949.

AN EPIDEMIC OF CRIPPLING STRIKES

Truman's woes with labor began only 18 days after he became President. Fractious John L. Lewis (shown below at right waving the mine safety code while haranguing a congressional committee) ordered 72,000 anthracite miners out of the pits. H.S.T. responded by using his wartime powers to put the affected mines under Government control. This did not stop Lewis who ordered two more strikes in 1946. A climactic showdown between the two men occurred in 1949 and 1950 when Lewis once again commanded his United Mine Workers to down tools. This time Truman, as the cartoon at right shows, finally applied muscle through the Taft-Hartley Act, a punitive labor law

that H.S.T. cordially disliked (he had vetoed it once, only to have it passed over his veto) but felt he had to employ to assure the wartime coal supply.

The United Steelworkers and their President Philip Murray *(below, left)* also plagued Truman, especially in 1952 when a strike stopped the flow of steel to Korean War armament manufacturers. As a last resort, Truman ordered the steel mills seized by the government. When the Supreme Court blocked this move as unconstitutional, the steel companies recovered control of their mills—and the workers immediately resumed a strike that was to last 55 days; the total loss in production and wages was estimated at $2.5 billion.

RAIL STRIKE: A PATTERN OF PARALYSIS

Dozens of trains stand idle in the Sunnyside Yards of the Long Island Railroad during the nation-wide rail stoppage of 1946. The strike was short-lived, but its legacy was widespread rancor. Truman forced a settlement by threatening government seizure of the roads. This convinced many union men that H.S.T. was anti-labor and the trainmen's union boss bitterly predicted that Truman had "signed his political death warrant." Truman never stood "against" labor; he understood that this strike, like the others, was a natural aftermath of wartime wage controls. Nonetheless, he saw his first duty in the preservation of a healthy economy.

A SHOOT-OUT WITH WOULD-BE ASSASSINS

Gunfire shattered the afternoon calm of Pennsylvania Avenue on November 1, 1950—and Truman was the target, the object of a tragic, futile assassination attempt. The gunmen, Oscar Collazo and Griselio Torresola, were fanatic Puerto Rican nationalists who believed Truman had "enslaved" their countrymen—although he had, in fact, done much to further Puerto Rican self-rule. When the two men attacked Blair House, the Presidential guest house where the Trumans were living while the White House was undergoing repairs, H.S.T. was in his bedroom taking a nap. Hearing gunfire, he leaped out of bed and rushed to the window to see what was going on, only getting out of the line of fire when a guard yelled at him. When the excitement was over, the President calmly kept a speaking engagement.

Undeterred by the assassination attempt,
Truman steps out on his usual morning walk.
The Secret Service did prevail on him to change
his ways after the shooting, insisting he walk
in secluded, easily policed parts of Washington.

Guard Donald Birdzell lies in the middle of
Pennsylvania Avenue *(far left)* bleeding from
wounds in both knees. He had run out in the
street to draw fire away from Blair House. Two
other guards were shot by the gunmen and
one, Leslie Coffelt, died of his wounds. Birdzell
is comforted by a passing motorist who bravely
stopped his car and jumped out to help.

The two would-be assassins lie near the door of
Blair House after being shot by guards, the
wounded Collazo at the foot of the front steps
(below) and the dead Torresola behind a nearby
hedge *(left)*. Amateur gunmen, the two had
simply tried to rush Blair House, blazing away
with pistols. Some 32 shots were exchanged,
many striking the Presidential residence.

Pudgy Whittaker Chambers *(left, in foreground)* testifies before the House Committee on Un-American Activities that Alger Hiss, a former State Department officer and a member of the U.S. mission to the U.N. Charter conference, was an active Communist in the 1930s. Later in the tense, dramatic hearings Hiss rose *(right)* to face his accuser and deny the charges.

HISS v. CHAMBERS: THE LOYALTY ISSUE

Few events of Truman's Presidency caused a greater stir in Washington and across the nation than the curious Hiss-Chambers affair. It began in 1948 when Whittaker Chambers, a confessed former Communist, accused Alger Hiss, a man who had held several high government posts, of subversion. Chambers said that Hiss had been a member of the Communist Party and had tried to pass a number of secret documents to Russia. Hiss labeled the charges "complete fabrications," but the Justice Department thought Hiss's denial a lie and indicted him for perjury. He was tried in 1950, found guilty and sent to jail. The whole affair thickened an atmosphere of suspicion, roiled by charges and countercharges of espionage and disloyalty, that gripped the country in the late 1940s and early 1950s—culminating in the dreadful years of fear and hysteria called the McCarthy Era. President Truman and his administration did not escape. They were charged with being "soft on Communism" and with tolerating lax security measures—although the reverse was true—and the issue continued to plague H.S.T. through his last four years in the White House.

A CARTOON CHRONICLE
OF TRUMAN'S TROUBLES

As Truman had his share of troubles in both foreign and domestic affairs, so he had his share of criticism from the press—and especially from newspaper cartoonists. A representative selection of these artistic brickbats, covering most of Truman's time in the Presidency, is shown on these pages. **1.** This 1950 cartoon correctly portrays Truman's chagrin at being "married" to the Taft-Hartley Act, a measure (passed over his veto) that he felt would foster, rather than cure, labor-management unrest. **2.** Truman's supposed penchant for making unguarded remarks at his press conferences is lampooned in this drawing from the anti-Truman Hearst press. **3.** A 1948 cartoon overestimates the threat to H.S.T. in that year's election by the Dixiecrat revolt in the previously solid Democratic South. **4.** Truman's statement in 1948 that the Republican charges of Soviet subversion were a "red herring" returned to plague him in such unkind cartoons as this one. **5.** Another pen and ink editorial from the election year of 1948 accurately mirrors H.S.T.'s troubles with large segments of the Democratic Party that had always staunchly backed Roosevelt. **6.** In a variation on a favorite theme, a worried Truman seeks to curb his own frankness with the press. **7.** This witty 1949 drawing makes whimsical fun of the fact that Truman was hesitant to use the Taft-Hartley Act he had vetoed to deal with John L. Lewis and his striking mineworkers. **8.** This drawing, which portrays Congress as a slow, elderly carpenter, lampoons the legislative delays that held up Truman's housing bill of 1949. **9.** Unkind comment on Truman's Presidency continued even after Eisenhower's election in 1952, as this departing Republican blast demonstrates.

4. A WHALE OF A HERRING!

2. CLASSIFIED!

3. HUMPTY DUMPTY

5. HOW DID FRANKLIN DO IT?

6. BEFORE A PRESS CONFERENCE

7. TREED

8.

9. TEACHER AND PUPIL

THE FIRST FAMILY OFF DUTY

5

On or off the job, Harry Truman always seemed to be having a whale of a time. When he could find a few hours or days of free time, he threw himself into having fun with all of his characteristic verve and bounce. He was by all odds the most informal and ebullient President in this century.

Margaret, too, always seemed to be enjoying herself, not allowing the fact that she was the President's daughter to restrict her social life or to keep her from launching a career as a concert singer. It was Bess Truman, doubtless, who suffered most from the pressures and the lack of privacy that go with life in the White House. She was stiffly embarrassed when forced to sit on the platform during political powwows and not much more at ease when opening charity bazaars or christening an Air Force plane, although she did these things with doughty determination. But she also managed some private fun, visiting her many close friends and attending athletic events.

The Trumans could escape protocol and relax best during their twice-yearly vacations at Key West, Florida. Truman chose Key West partly because of its climate and partly because the Navy's submarine base there possessed the communications equipment needed to keep him in close and secret touch with Washington. But at Key West he wore the inescapable burdens of office lightly, swimming a lot, fishing occasionally and setting a new Presidential style in the freewheeling informality of his attire.

Listening to music and playing the piano were other favorite forms of relaxation for H.S.T., and a part of this preoccupation was his daughter's career as a concert singer. These activities and interests occasionally earned him a bad press. Although Truman was a quite competent musician, the Republicans professed to find it ridiculous to have a piano-playing President. (One anti-Truman gag was a revival of the vaudeville comedian's old plea: "Don't shoot the piano player, boys. He's doing the best he can.") His spirited defense of Margaret when a Washington music critic panned her singing got further unwelcome attention in the press (page 104). Truman did not enjoy such carping at his activities, but he did not let it cramp his style. He seldom refrained from doing, wearing and saying pretty much what he pleased when he felt he was off duty.

Performing an annual rite, President Truman prepares to open the 1952 baseball season by throwing out the first ball. Truman always enjoyed the ceremony, joking with players and bystanders about his baseball prowess—and usually managing to fling the ball about 30 feet. Bess Truman was the family's real ball fan and often took parties of her women friends with her to Washington Senators games.

LAUGHTER AT KEY WEST

One of the chief joys of Key West vacations for the President was the chance they gave him to be with his wife and daughter in a more relaxed atmosphere than prevailed at the White House. Though the Trumans were still in the public eye, the protocol—not to mention the heavy work routine—of life in Washington could be shucked off. Vacations also gave Truman a chance to talk quietly with such old friends as Chief Justice Fred Vinson, who visited often, away from the clatter of government. And they gave him the chance to wear the comfortable, flashy duds that outraged clothing manufacturers and other arbiters of taste.

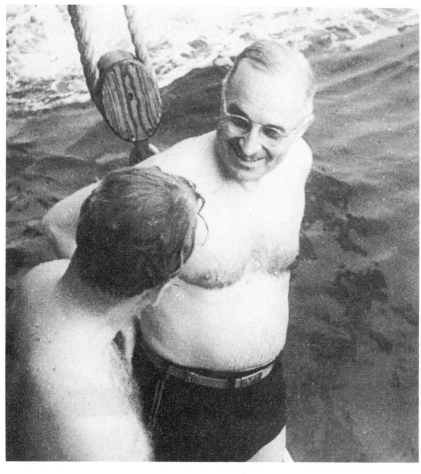

Truman chats with an aide on the deck of the Presidential yacht *Williamsburg* after taking a dip in the warm waters of the Caribbean. A good swimmer, Truman developed his own versions of the side and breast strokes to keep his head out of water and his glasses dry. When not on vacation, Truman frequently used the graceful 244-foot *Williamsburg* for short weekend cruises on the Potomac River.

Truman jokes with reporters during an informal press conference at Key West in the spring of 1951. Such conferences were kept to a minimum while Truman was on vacation.

The Trumans—Margaret at far left, Bess to the President's right—laugh heartily with friends and aides as a comic parade cooked up by the Key West press corps passes the "Winter White House." Truman, relaxing after his come-from-behind election victory in 1948, was in high good humor although this vacation, more than most, involved work—he and his advisers had to prepare the 1949 message to Congress that would kick off the new administration.

TRYING THE TRADITIONAL PASTIMES

Save for the fedora hat, Harry Truman looks the part of an authentic hunter in the picture at left, taken at a hunting camp in Sibley, Missouri. His companions, as usual, are old and close friends, in this case Judge E. I. Purcell, who served with Truman on the Jackson County Court, and Eddie Jacobson, Truman's partner in the short-lived Kansas City haberdashery. Actually, Truman was never much of a hunter. Although a good shot with both rifle and pistol, he always hated to kill animals. The hunting camp's poker games were more to his liking.

66 . . . *I do not like to hunt animals and I never have. I do not believe in shooting at anything that cannot shoot back.* 99 —Harry S. Truman

Truman grins broadly at a reporter as a Secret Service man weighs the "Truman Team's" catch on a dock at Key West during a fishing contest between press and Presidential staff. Truman was not much more of a fisherman than he was a hunter, and for the same reason: he never liked to kill anything. (As a boy he often read books while his friends fished Independence's Little Blue River.) At Key West he liked to go out on the water, but seldom put a line overboard.

66*Harry is a good poker player. He can take care of himself . . . [but] he isn't much of a fisherman . . . he always said that the reason he never caught any fish was that he didn't like fish to eat.* 99 —Eddie Jacobson

KEY WEST FISHING CAP

THE USUAL SOFT STETSON

HONORARY DEGREE MORTARBOARD

VETERANS' OVERSEAS CAP

THE SUMMER PANAMA

A HAT FOR EVERY OCCASION

Truman became famous not only for his informal and even gaudy vacation clothes, but also for the astonishing variety of his hats. His normal headgear was the wide-brimmed fedora he is shown wearing in the large photograph at left. He was also partial to caps and wore a number of styles when vacationing or on sea voyages. And like any President, he had to attend a multitude of official or semi-official functions that called for still other sorts of headgear, such as the fez *(bottom)* he wore to a Shriner Convention.

SEAGOING TWEED CAP

OXFORD DEGREE VELVET TAM

PITH HELMET FOR KEY WEST

SHRINER'S FEZ

DIPLOMATIC TOPPER

VACATIONER'S CLOTH CAP

MUSIC–WITH A SOUR NOTE

Truman sincerely enjoyed music, both as listener and participant. Occasionally his love of the piano, and his willingness to play it in public, got him into trouble. While he was Vice President, Truman attended a party at Washington's National Press Club. Urged to play, he obliged—only to have Lauren Bacall, newly famous for her sexy role in the Humphrey Bogart film *To Have and Have Not*, perch leggily on top of the piano. The resulting picture, printed across the nation, did little to convince the public that Truman was a tower of dignity. He came off much better on another musical occasion in 1958, after leaving the White House, when he was guest conductor of the Kansas City Philharmonic *(right)*. He conducted, one critic reported, "briskly and sedately."

THE FUROR OVER MARGARET'S VOICE

Margaret Truman, as musically inclined as her father, launched her career as a concert singer in 1947. (She is seen at right taking a bow after an early concert in Pittsburgh.) Truman naturally followed his daughter's progress with great eagerness and parental pride. It was this protective fatherly concern that caused one of the most famous incidents of Truman's Presidency. On Tuesday evening, December 5, 1950, Margaret sang in Constitution Hall in Washington, D.C. Her concert was stingingly reviewed by Paul Hume (*above*), the perfectionist music critic of *The Washington Post*. Outraged by the review, Truman dashed off a hand-written and exceedingly ill-tempered note to Hume on White House stationery. Word of the letter, and eventually its text, got out, and Truman was severely condemned for his vulgarity. What few people took into consideration was the great strain on Truman at the time. China had recently entered the Korean War, and its divisions were pouring across the Manchurian border. The very evening of the concert Charles Ross, Truman's Press Secretary and lifelong friend, had died at his desk of a heart attack. December 5 was, perhaps, the blackest day of Truman's entire Presidency. Critic Hume was one of the few people to respond to Truman's letter with fitting charity: "I can only say that a man suffering the loss of a close friend and carrying the terrible burden of the present world crisis ought to be indulged in an occasional outburst of temper."

WHAT CRITIC PAUL HUME WROTE

Margaret Truman, soprano, sang at Constitution Hall last night. It was not her first recital there, and it probably was not her last. Miss Truman is a unique American phenomenon with a pleasant voice of little size and fair quality.

She is extremely attractive on the stage. Her program is usually light in nature, designed to attract those who like the singing of Jeanette MacDonald and Nelson Eddy. Yet Miss Truman can-

not sing very well.

She is flat a good deal of the time—more last night than at any time we have heard her in past years. There are few moments during her recital when one can relax and feel confident that she will make her goal, which is the end of the song.

Miss Truman has not improved in the years we have heard her. . . . She has learned that she must work in order to make something of her voice. But she still cannot sing with anything approaching professional finish. . . .

It is an extremely unpleasant duty to record such unhappy facts about so honestly appealing a person. But as long as Miss Truman sings as she has for three years, and does today, we seem to have no recourse unless it is to omit comment on her programs altogether.

THE NOTE, SIGNED "H. S. T.," THAT TRUMAN WROTE HUME

Mr. Hume—

I have just read your lousy review of Margaret's concert. I've come to the conclusion that you are an "eight ulcer man on four ulcer pay."

It seems to me that you are a frustrated old man who wishes he could have been successful. When you write such poppycock . . . it shows conclusively that you're off the beam and at least four of your ulcers are at work. Someday I hope to meet you. When that happens you'll need a new nose, a lot of beefsteak for black eyes and perhaps a supporter below.

[Columnist Westbrook] Pegler, a guttersnipe, is a gentleman alongside you. I hope you'll accept that statement as a worse insult than a reflection on your ancestry.

Margaret accepts a bouquet of roses from Karl Krueger, conductor of the Detroit Symphony Orchestra, after her singing debut on March 16, 1947. The U.S. public was surprised to find a President's daughter striking out on a career of her own.

A SHY FIRST LADY
GETTING SOME
UNWONTED ATTENTION

Bess Truman gasps as clown Emmet Kelly makes
her the center of his act during a 1946 benefit
performance of the Ringling Bros. and Barnum
& Bailey Circus. The First Lady attended the
circus with a group of her oldest friends, the
Tuesday Bridge Club of Independence, whom
she had invited to visit Washington.

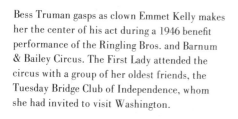

The sequence of pictures on these two pages is from a newsreel that delighted the nation in 1945—and very likely dismayed Mrs. Truman. She is shown attempting with hearty determination but little success to christen an airplane by breaking a bottle of champagne over its nose. The best girl tennis player in Independence in her youth, Mrs. Truman's swing did not lack vigor, as the top two pictures at left and the bottom two below amply prove, but the bottle simply would not break. An Air Force major came to her aid, first by showing her a better aiming point on the aircraft's nose *(below)*. Finally he gallantly took over as bottle breaker *(right)* but with no better luck.

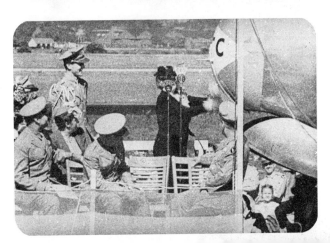

THE DAILY STINT
OF EXERCISE

Vacations at Key West, music, family doings—all
these helped Truman carry the enormous burdens of
the Presidency. Perhaps even more important was Truman's insistence on a daily break for exercise. Usually
it was an early morning walk; these walks, in fact, became a Truman trademark. An early riser always, he
set out at 6:30 a.m. and covered a mile and a half before 7. When bad weather or an emergency made a
morning walk impossible, he managed to squeeze in
some calisthenics or a swim in the White House pool.
All this activity amused reporters who often made
light of it in their stories, but it seems to have
worked. Few Presidents in their 60s have been as chipper as Truman and few seemed to age less in office.

Truman steps out on his morning walk in Independence, as usual
leaving news photographers scattered in his wake. He always
walked at a vigorous 120 steps to the minute—the U.S. Army's
official marching cadence. The President denied that his fast pace
was intended to exhaust the press. His straightforward dictum:
". . . if you are going to walk for your physical benefit, it is
necessary that you walk as if you are going some place."

A grinning Truman does knee bends on the main deck of the
battleship U.S.S. *Missouri* during a diplomatic trip to Brazil
in September 1947. The T-shirt was given him by the White House
reporters, who invented the "Truman Athletic Club" and named
the President the club's "coach." The shirt also had six stars
on the sleeves in joking reference to the fact that as Commander-in-
Chief, the President outranks even a five-star general.

★ ★ ★ ★
FINAL

DAILY NEWS

Copr. 1950 by News Syndicate Co. Inc. **NEW YORK'S** **PICTURE NEWSPAPER** Trade Mark Reg. U. S. Pat. Off.

3¢

Vol. 32. No. 3   New York 17, Wednesday, June 28, 1950★   88 Main+12 Brooklyn+8 Kings Pages   3 Cents IN CITY LIMITS | 4 CENTS in Suburbs | 5 CENTS Elsewhere

U. S. FLIERS RIP KOREAN REDS; UN OKs FORCE

MacArthur Acts on Truman Order

—Stories on page **3**

Approaching the Problem. A serious-visaged President Truman, flanked by grim Attorney General J. Howard McGrath (left) and Defense Secretary Louis Johnson, walks from Blair House to White House to plan latest moves in Korean crisis. Following orders from Truman, U. S. planes went into action in Korea. (Associated Press Wirefoto)

HARD, FATEFUL DECISIONS
IN A BLOODY, TRAGIC WAR

6

President Truman's last two and a half years in office were shadowed by the bloody Korean War and by the many difficult and fateful decisions it entailed. It all began when Truman was informed on Saturday, June 24, 1950, that the army of Communist North Korea (largely Russian-trained and -equipped) had smashed southward across the 38th parallel, the border established after World War II between North Korea and the Republic of South Korea. It was quickly evident that the South Korean army, as yet only partially trained by its U.S. military advisers, was no match for the invaders. Truman made up his mind immediately: although fully aware that he might be triggering World War III, he resolved to send U.S. forces to help the South Koreans. The United Nations, in a historic resolution, pledged its support.

American troops were soon engaged in desperate rear-guard actions to preserve a foothold on the Korean peninsula. Whole divisions with their equipment and supplies poured across the Pacific in one of the swiftest military buildups ever seen. By August the North Korean advance had been slowed and a front stabilized, defending the port of Pusan. Then, on September 15, General Douglas MacArthur, U.S. commander in the Far East (and commander of all U.N. forces in Korea), executed one of history's most daring maneuvers, landing a large amphibious force at Inchon, well up Korea's west coast and some 150 miles in the rear of the enemy troops. Outflanked and cut off from their supply sources, the North Koreans, who had seemed to have the whole country in their grasp, were forced to flee northward. So smashing was the victory that by October 30, only four months after the fighting had begun, a national magazine could print the headline, "Hard-Hitting U.N. Forces Wind Up War."

Then came a ghastly reversal. General MacArthur, authorized by Washington to proceed north of the 38th parallel, was told to move ahead prudently so as not to give China unnecessary cause for alarm. Instead he gave his armies their head, and they dashed toward the Yalu River, the border between North Korea and Communist China's province of Manchuria. The Chinese responded—in overwhelming force. Some 200,000 well-equipped and suicidally determined Chinese troops fell on the U.N. forces, which reeled backward suffering terrible losses. As his troops retreated, MacArthur repeatedly—and publicly—demanded to be allowed to bomb targets in Manchuria and elsewhere in China. Such an enlargement of the war was completely counter to the policy determined by Truman and his advisers, and the President was forced to make another fateful decision: to fire a general who had become a popular idol.

After this climactic series of episodes, the war settled down into an agonizing and deadly stalemate. As the conflict dragged on, Truman came to one of the last momentous steps of his Presidency: the decision not to run for another term, to relinquish to someone else the terrible burdens of war and the Presidency.

This front page from the New York *Daily News* dated June 28, 1950, vividly summarizes the first urgent days of the Korean War. Word of the North Korean invasion had reached Truman on June 24; quickly the President had resolved to intervene, had ordered U.S. planes to strafe the invaders and had pushed a resolution through the U.N. calling for armed assistance to South Korea.

SWIFT, MOMENTOUS MOVES TO AID SOUTH KOREA

Reporters crowd a White House press room on June 27, 1950, flashing word to their papers of Truman's decision to intervene in Korea. On that day (a Tuesday) the President announced that he had ordered U.S. air and naval units to give the South Korean troops whatever help they could. Early Friday morning, informed by MacArthur that the South Korean army would collapse unless given further aid, Truman gave the order to start moving U.S. infantry units from Japan to the Korean peninsula.

Taking a historic step, U.S. Ambassador to the United Nations Warren R. Austin and British representative Sir Terence Shone raise their arms to signal an emphatic "yea" to the resolution, introduced by the U.S., urging members of the international body to aid South Korea. The U.N. Security Council was able to pass the resolution only because Russia, which would otherwise have exercised its veto, was not taking part in Council meetings. It was then boycotting the U.N. for its refusal to seat Red China. The empty U.S.S.R. seat is at far left.

AGONY AND DEATH
IN ASIA

The Korean War was a very tough, very bloody and extremely frustrating conflict. The first U.S. troops to be sent from Japan had to face Russian-built T-34 tanks without any tanks of their own or even antitank weapons, and they took a terrible shellacking. Later, when hordes of Chinese troops poured down out of Manchuria, U.N. forces again had to struggle back across the rugged Korean landscape, this time in the depths of an incredibly cold winter. Before the conflict was over, the United States forces alone had suffered 157,530 casualties: 33,629 killed in battle, 20,617 dead from accidents and disease, and 103,284 wounded.

A Marine corporal *(left)* weeps after his squad has been virtually annihilated; another soldier *(below)* cradles the head of a comrade who mourns the death of a friend. These moments of agony occurred in the early months of the war when the first detachments of U.S. troops sent to Korea were trying to bolster the South Korean forces and preserve a beachhead. The photograph at lower left shows the horrors of the retreat that followed China's entry into the war, as a detachment of Marines files down a road known as "Nightmare Alley" past the mangled bodies of other U.S. troops who had been ambushed by Chinese infantry.

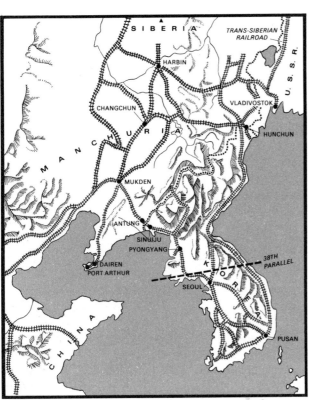

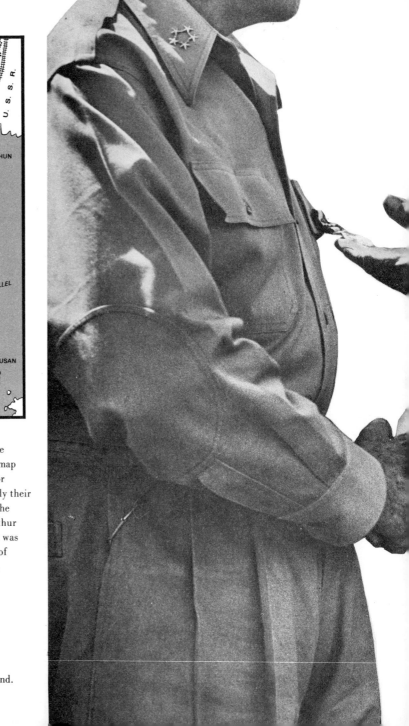

A key to the Chinese intervention in the Korean War and to the Truman-MacArthur controversy that followed is shown in the map above—the extensive rail network of Korea's northern neighbor Manchuria. It was these railroads that helped the Chinese supply their invading armies and reverse the course of the war. And it was the Manchurian supply lines, along with other targets, that MacArthur wanted to bomb, thus crippling the Chinese war effort. Truman was unalterably opposed to widening the war by attacking any part of China, however strategically advisable such an attack might be.

Truman congratulates MacArthur as he awards the general the Distinguished Service Cross during their meeting on Wake Island.

QUIET PRELUDE
TO A NOISY CRISIS

Shortly after the U.N. forces crossed the 38th parallel in pursuit of the North Korean army, Truman decided it was time to speak to his victorious (but often head-strong) field commander in person. The two men met on Wake Island on October 15, 1950, and their two conferences were informal, friendly and brief. The most vital question Truman asked the general was, "What are the chances for Chinese or Soviet interference in the Korean fighting?" MacArthur replied that he had reports of more than 300,000 Chinese troops in Manchuria, but he did not think they would attack.

This was a fatal miscalculation. As Truman bitterly observed some time later, "I traveled 14,000 miles to Wake Island to get a lot of misinformation." For the President, this was the first of a chain of events that was to culminate in the decision to relieve MacArthur of his command. In H.S.T.'s view, it was not only that MacArthur repeatedly asked the President and the Joint Chiefs of Staff for permission to bomb Chinese targets and in other ways escalate the war. It was also that MacArthur pressed his views publicly in various messages and communiques. Truman exploded with rage at such insubordination, privately saying, "Who the hell does he think he is—God?" But he held his hand until April 11, 1951, when, in a soberly worded statement, he replaced MacArthur with General Matthew B. Ridgway. Truman's action caused a furor among the senior general's many admirers and the President was noisily vilified. But as Truman saw it, he had little choice. The U.S. Constitution makes the President Commander-in-Chief of the armed forces and subordinates those forces to the civilian government. No Commander-in-Chief can tolerate a general who publicly challenges the decisions of that government. MacArthur and his supporters rejected this argument, and the general remained convinced to the end of his life that he had done nothing wrong and that only malice lay behind his firing.

THE DISMISSAL OF AN IDOL

Reveille

YOU'RE PRESIDENT OF THE UNITED STATES!

ASIA POLICY CRISIS

MACARTHUR DEMANDS

CAPT. HARRY TRUMAN

HERBLOCK

REVEILLE—FROM "THE HERBLOCK BOOK" (BEACON PRESS, 1951)

A pointed Herblock cartoon, printed in *The Washington Post* on the
very morning Truman relieved MacArthur, sums up the feelings of
the many Americans who thought that the President should have
fired the outspoken general sooner than he did.

A grim-faced MacArthur prepares to leave Tokyo, his headquarters
since the end of World War II. Among the devoted aides who
accompanied the general were Colonel Sidney Huff, wiping his eye,
and Major General Courtney Whitney *(far right)*. MacArthur's
successor, General Ridgway, stands by MacArthur's left shoulder.

66*. . . in exercising his constitutional power to relieve me Mr. Truman
did so in a way which amounted to drastic summary punishment. . . .
This was no mere change of command. It was a vengeful reprisal.***99**
—General Douglas MacArthur

A LAST CHANGE OF COMMAND

Harry Truman announced that he would not seek another term as President at a Jefferson-Jackson Day dinner in Washington on March 29, 1952. The 5,300 Democrats present were stunned, but it was not a sudden decision on Truman's part. As early as November 1951, he had told his staff, swearing them to secrecy. One reason he gave publicly was that he had served almost all of two terms and that two terms were enough for any President. But in private he confessed the job was a "man-killer" and once said he did not "want to be carried out of the White House in a pine box."

Truman announces his decision not to run again to a shocked audience of Democrats. His surprise announcement was not part of his prepared speech. For secrecy's sake, Truman had written it out in longhand *(below)* and interpolated the statement into his 30-minute address.

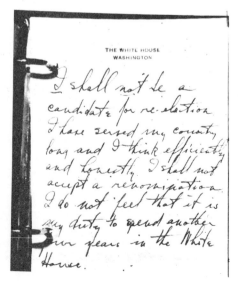

THE WHITE HOUSE
WASHINGTON

I shall not be a candidate for re-election I have served my country long and I think efficiently and honestly I shall not accept a renomination I do not feel that it is my duty to spend another four years in the White House.

At a White House conference with Truman
shortly after the election, President-elect Dwight
D. Eisenhower listens tensely as the two chat
for the photographers. Personal relations
between the two men, never very cordial,
worsened at this meeting: Truman felt that
Eisenhower should join him in reassuring the
world that U.S. foreign policy objectives (e.g.,
no forcible repatriation for Korean War
prisoners) would be continued after the
succession; Ike was edgy about being pinned
down on policy before he could assume office.

BUSY, VIGOROUS
YEARS OF RETIREMENT

Harry Truman was never so popular as he was in retirement. Nine thousand people crammed Washington's Union Station to see the Trumans off on the train that took them home to Independence, and so many women managed to kiss the new ex-President that his face was entirely covered with lipstick. A crowd of 10,000 greeted them at the Independence railroad station, and some 5,000 more somehow jammed themselves in front of the Truman home. Truman managed a short speech, but Mrs. Truman was too moved to utter a word until they had gotten inside their front door. Then she said, "If this is what you get for all those years of hard work I guess it was worth it." Even newspapers that had long lambasted Truman suddenly changed their tune and acknowledged that the man who had just stepped down from the Presidency had been a hard-working and devoted servant of the American people. As Truman said, "Some editors ate crow and left the feathers on."

Retirement for a man with Truman's energy and drive did not mean getting up late and loafing. He rose early, as always, took his vigorous walk, studied the newspapers and kept up a voluminous correspondence. He also found to his delight that after years of being surrounded by servants and Secret Service men he was once again able to do things for himself like carrying suitcases, buying train tickets and driving a car. In addition, retirement gave Truman a chance to achieve a pair of serious ambitions—to write a long, factual account of his Presidency in his *Memoirs*, and to establish a Truman Library where his papers and those of other Presidents could be stored and studied. Best of all, perhaps, Truman could look back with satisfaction on his achievements in office. Among his memories, he could ponder what is surely one of the greatest compliments ever paid one world leader by another. The scene was a conference between Truman and Winston Churchill aboard the yacht *Williamsburg* shortly before Truman's term in office expired. Churchill looked up at Truman and said, "I must confess, sir, I held you in very low regard . . . [at Potsdam]. I loathed your taking the place of Franklin Roosevelt." Then Churchill went on: "I misjudged you badly. Since that time, you, more than any other man, have saved Western Civilization."

Harry and Bess Truman proudly stand in front of their comfortable
14-room house on North Delaware Avenue in Independence after
Truman's retirement. The house, built more than 100 years ago by
Mrs. Truman's grandfather, was her home as a girl and is still
known to older townspeople as "the Wallace House."

THE PLEASURES
OF LIFE
IN INDEPENDENCE

Mrs. Truman picks roses from a trellis in back of the family house while the ex-President performs his morning ritual of picking up the papers the delivery boy has flung over the fence. Insatiably interested and curious, as always, Truman in retirement continued to take a half dozen newspapers—"you cannot get all the facts from just one"—and he studied them hard. But if he was intensely interested in what was going on in the outside world, and especially in politics, Truman, like his wife, was also heartily glad to be back in their small, handsome hometown of Independence, one of whose tree-shaded streets is seen at left. "When you live in a big town," Truman once said, "you get to know very few people. It is almost the same as living in the desert."

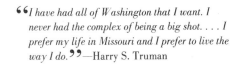

I have had all of Washington that I want. I never had the complex of being a big shot. . . . I prefer my life in Missouri and I prefer to live the way I do.—Harry S. Truman

MARRIAGE FOR HIS ONLY CHILD

The Trumans meet the Daniels on the front
walk of the Truman home in April 1956, shortly
before Margaret and Clifton Daniel Jr.
(below, center) were married. Below right are
his parents, Mr. and Mrs. E. Clifton Daniel.

Truman at times had expressed his concern
that Margaret might repeat a pattern followed
by many women in the Truman family, including
his own sister, and remain single. So he was
delighted with her decision at age 32 to get
married, although he looks as nervously grim
in the picture at left as most fathers do
when they escort their daughters to the church.
The wedding, held in Independence's small
Trinity Church, naturally drew a large crowd
of onlookers who applauded when Margaret
and her new husband emerged after the
ceremony *(right)*. Clifton Daniel, whom Margaret
had met while living in New York, was then a
reporter for *The New York Times* and later
became the paper's managing editor.

A STRONG, PERSISTENT VOICE
IN DEMOCRATIC POLITICS

Despite retirement, Truman leaped into the fray when the 1956 and 1960 elections came around. In 1956 he "opened up a political hornet's nest" by backing Averell Harriman for the nomination rather than Adlai Stevenson (whom Truman had picked as his successor in 1952) because he felt Stevenson was incapable of fighting a tough, winning campaign. This temporarily estranged Truman from Stevenson and from Stevenson's most loyal backer, Mrs. Roosevelt, shown together at lower left. But when the 1956 convention chose Stevenson, Truman gave a speech (left) pledging his support. In 1961 John Kennedy gave a dinner in the White House for the former President and his family (below).

A HAPPY, RELAXED TOUR OF EUROPE

Truman (wearing a handsome Oxford University robe and velvet hat) and his wife beam with delight during one of the high points of their 1956 trip to Europe—the bestowal on the former President of Oxford's honorary degree of Doctor of Civil Law. Shortly after Margaret's marriage, the Trumans took off for a leisurely tour of England and the Continent. They were accompanied by Judge Samuel Rosenman, a long-time friend and adviser, and Mrs. Rosenman, and they enjoyed themselves thoroughly. The trip included a warm reunion with Sir Winston and Lady Churchill, a visit to the French Riviera where Truman enjoyed browsing about the cobbled streets of the ancient village of Eze *(far right)* and an interview with painter Pablo Picasso whose gregarious personality was right in tune with Truman's. H.S.T.'s popularity abroad was evident in the warm welcomes he and his party received everywhere. The Oxford students were especially demonstrative. Truman's first name was latinized as "Harricum" on his degree parchment; the students, remembering the 1948 election, cheerfully greeted him with shouts of "Give 'em hell, Harricum!" The University Orator also remembered 1948. The speech that accompanied the award of Truman's degree included a Latin verse, adapted from Virgil, describing the plight of H.S.T.'s opponents in that year. The verse, and a translation, are given below.

"Heu vatum ignarae mentes! quid vota repulsum, quid promisa invant? tua quid praesagia, Gallup?"

(The seers saw not defeat, poor souls, Vain prayers, vain promises, vain Gallup poll!)

THE PROUDEST OF PROUD GRANDFATHERS

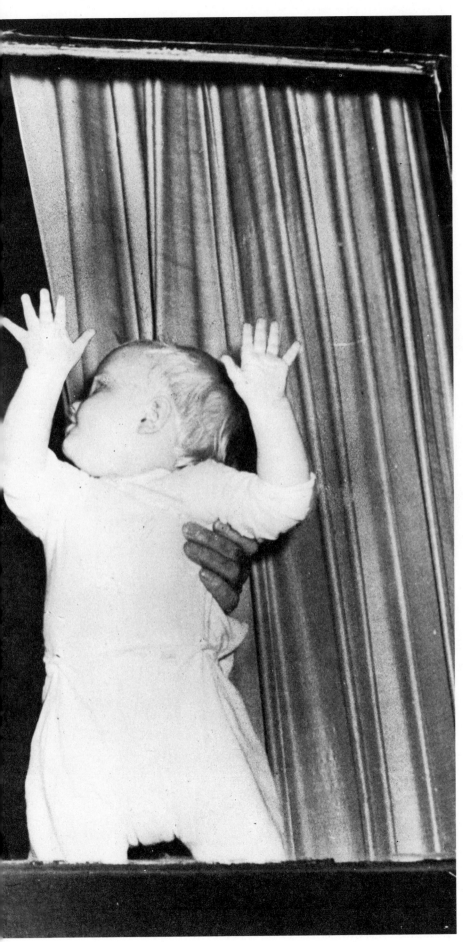

Harry Truman happily holds up his two grandsons, Clifton Truman Daniel and William Wallace Daniel, in the window of his daughter Margaret's New York apartment in April 1960. That spring Margaret and her husband themselves took a trip to Europe, and the proud grandparents were delighted to pitch in and babysit. Young Clifton was then almost three years old, his younger brother almost one. Truman, who had had but one daughter, was especially pleased to have a pair of grandsons. During this visit Truman, as always, took his morning walks; he was followed, as always, by newsmen and—as always—made a number of salty remarks. The newsmen confirmed that Truman was opposed to the nomination of John F. Kennedy in 1960 because he thought J.F.K. too young and too much under the influence of his powerful father, Joseph P. Kennedy, whom Truman had always disliked. For H.S.T., the young Kennedy's Roman Catholicism was not a factor. "It's not the Pope who worries me," Truman explained, "it's the pop."

FITTING LEGACY: THE TRUMAN LIBRARY

The Truman Library, with its curving 525-foot
façade, lies on the outskirts of Independence, a
short walk from Truman's house. Dedicated
in 1957, it is made of white Indiana limestone
and cost about two million dollars.

The great project of Truman's years of retirement
was to establish a library that would house his Presidential papers and also serve as a collecting point
for material on other Presidents. Truman knew, both
as an omnivorous reader of history and as a former
President, that the nature of the Presidency had never received sufficient study. While he was President,
Truman had persuaded Congress to appropriate funds
for the collecting and cataloging of past Presidents' papers—which had never been done before. Now, he
gave his library, which was built with money con-
tributed by thousands of friends, an estimated 3.5
million documents from his own Presidential files and
from the files of political associates. He also arranged
for the National Archives to operate the library and
to begin making a microfilm collection of the papers
of previous Chief Executives. No more fitting memorial can be imagined for a man whose decisions were
so often based on his profound reading of the past
and who was, although he had no university education, one of the nation's few scholar-Presidents.

Truman joins Thomas Hart Benton beneath a
mural Benton painted for the library *(right)*. So
much memorabilia poured in that some, such as
the items above—including a bust and a
caricature of H.S.T.—remained in storage.

Approaching his 86th birthday, former President Harry Truman walks with a cane toward his house after a shopping trip. Behind Truman is his car with Missouri license place number 5-745, which stands for the date when Germany surrendered at the end of World War II, May 7, 1945. Truman was President at the time and has had the same license plates every year since he has been out of the White House.

AN HISTORIAN'S VIEW
OF HARRY TRUMAN'S PRESIDENCY

8

by D.W. Brogan

From the beginning, the office of Vice President of the United States has seemed to nearly all its incumbents futile and to most of them disillusioning. The only real attraction of the office (except for a naturally lazy man) is the possibility of succeeding to the Presidency on the death of the President. This has happened eight times. Lyndon B. Johnson is too much part of current history for his role to be assessed even tentatively, but of the other Vice Presidents who have succeeded, only two can have any claims to be considered great Presidents. One of them was Theodore Roosevelt; the other was Harry S. Truman.

From the moment that the sudden death of Franklin D. Roosevelt made Harry Truman the center of American power, the new President was involved in issues of the highest importance. Not all of his decisions can be justified, and some have been severely criticized. But from the first Mr. Truman showed the essential qualities of a President: the willingness to take responsibility and to decide rapidly. His motto, "the buck stops here," is the essential aspect of the Presidential office.

In the light of history, perhaps the most important act performed by the new President was the decision to drop the atomic bomb, a weapon of whose existence he knew nothing when he became President. That decision has been much debated, especially the resolve to drop the bomb on densely populated cities like Hiroshima and Nagasaki; but it was made. For good or ill, Truman was the President who opened Pandora's box by deciding to bomb Hiroshima. Both Truman and Churchill looked on the bomb as a providential weapon to end the war with Japan; without the bomb, their military advisers calculated that Japan would have to be invaded, with the possible loss of a million Allied lives. Truman solicited the counsel of his top scientific, military and civilian advisers, but he has clearly stated that the final decision and responsibility were his. For as an enthusiastic student of American history, Mr. Truman knew that on him, and on him alone, lay the ultimate responsibility of any great decision of the President and Commander-in-Chief of the United States.

Truman did not look back. Having determined to drop the atomic bomb on Japan, he did not stay awake nights. Whether the decision was justifiable, whether the demonstration of the new power of destruction could have been made in another way, are still matters of bitter dispute. But Mr. Truman accepted re-

Students representing Truman High School in Independence, Missouri, present former President Harry S. Truman (left) with a special birthday card on the occasion of his 86th birthday, May 8, 1970.

sponsibility for what he did, apparently without regrets or pangs of conscience.

For the nearly eight years that Mr. Truman was in office, this power of decision was the most important power to have. For it was essential that the United States should be, and should seem to be, under firm command, even if not all the examples of the command were encouraging or successful. For this reason Mr. Truman will go down to history as one who maintained the power as well as the dignity of the Presidential office. He is in the line of Chief Executives who used Presidential power sometimes outside, if not quite against, the letter of the Constitution—the line of Jefferson buying Louisiana, Jackson facing down the revolt of South Carolina, Lincoln deciding, as finally he alone decided, to open the Civil War by replying in arms to the firing on Fort Sumter. Truman repeatedly demonstrated his readiness to use his power, perhaps most notably by moving quickly and decisively when South Korea was invaded, without waiting for full Congressional debate and declaration of war.

At the time he took office this power of decision was not immediately visible. Mr. Truman was thought of as a very accidental President—indeed, as having been an accidental Vice President (F.D.R. passed over several more impressive candidates for that office in 1944). He even showed in his early days some regard for the old hierarchy by nominating a Senate leader whom he admired, James F. Byrnes, as Secretary of State. He asked for advice from elder statesmen like Henry Stimson; he took advice. But it soon became apparent that he was fully conscious that he was President and that the buck stopped with him.

In part, this was the result of the educational impact of the office he had inherited. When Winston Churchill was asked why his successor, that very undramatic figure Clement Attlee, had shown himself so authoritative a Prime Minister, Churchill replied that he had fed "on the Royal Jelly." But of course both Truman and Attlee were men whose basic qualities had been hidden in minor offices and were revealed only when each man was stretched to his fullness. That each had been a successful fighting officer commanding men in the field is perhaps significant in assessing their later roles.

There were other aspects in the new President's career that were perhaps more useful to him than his experience as a captain of field artillery on the Western Front in 1918, although that was an experience he liked to dwell on. He had been put into the Senate by the Pendergast machine in Kansas City, as he had been given his first political job by that machine, a job in which he combined executive efficiency with rigid honesty, a rare combination in the Kansas City of that age. It was these qualities of thoroughness and honesty that enabled Truman to live down, both at home and among his colleagues in the Senate, his first reputation of being merely a Pendergast stooge. Yet Truman preserved some of the habits of the Kansas City political world—particularly a deep loyalty to old friends that involved him indirectly in scandals, especially toward the end of his administration. But by that time people concentrated more on the loyalty he showed than on the indiscretion he displayed. He had by then earned on a national scale the trust he had earned long before in Kansas City.

Truman had not merely to live down the Pendergast machine, he had to live in the shadow of a great name, that of F.D.R. He inherited a great deal of unfinished business, and he inherited a Cabinet and other personnel chosen by a President who had been in office so long that many young Americans could not remember any other. It was natural for Truman to get rid of the Roosevelt Cabinet, but it was bitterly resented by many loyal New Dealers, especially those on the radical side like Henry A. Wallace.

The Roosevelt Cabinet and F.D.R.'s great administrative chiefs had been prima donnas. The Truman appointees, for the most part, were not. Yet at the end of his administration there could be no doubt that the Truman Cabinet was a more effective instrument of government and contained more useful public servants than the Roosevelt Cabinet had; more than that, the devotion of the

Cabinet (containing figures like Dean Acheson and Robert Lovett) to their chief was more manifest than the devotion of the Roosevelt Cabinet to F.D.R. And the relationship between President Truman and General George C. Marshall was far closer and mutually far more trusting than that between Roosevelt and Marshall. In this sense Truman was out of F.D.R.'s shadow long before he left the White House.

In another way, as well, Truman was out of the Roosevelt shadow. He was a great maker of the modern Presidency as a department of the nation's government in its own right.

The most that F.D.R. did was to improve, to some degree, the organization of the White House. But what Truman did was to improve very markedly, and impose discipline on, the whole organization of the executive branch of the United States government. In administrative history, despite the scandals and despite the errors, Mr. Truman will go down as a great innovator and reformer. There were few of the tense personal rivalries that had marked Roosevelt's Cabinets— with Roosevelt's approval, since F.D.R. believed that in the clash of personalities fresher ideas might be born. Instead Truman used his Cabinet to sift carefully ideas and approaches to problems. He also met frequently with the various committees and boards that operated within the executive branch, soliciting expert opinion before making his own decisions. He often asked that memoranda and position papers be formulated for his careful scrutiny. He brought into the White House such men as Clark Clifford and encouraged them to impose organizational efficiency on what had tended to be independent chaos. (Clifford, important as an adviser and strategist for Truman, remained a part-time adviser of Presidents John F. Kennedy and Lyndon B. Johnson, and became Secretary of Defense in Johnson's Cabinet.)

When Eisenhower succeeded to the Presidency, he inherited a much more effective instrument of command than had Truman.

But what did Truman do with this instrument of command? His accomplishments in the foreign field were substantial, but he was less lucky in domestic affairs. As always happens after a great war, the public was in the mood, consciously or unconsciously, to revenge itself on the government that had imposed such burdens on it. In addition, Truman found himself confronted with serious and disruptive postwar problems—strikes, rising prices, food and housing shortages—that were bound to antagonize the electorate. He dealt firmly with these problems, sending message after message to Congress asking for needed legislation. But Congress did not always give him the laws he felt he needed to meet the onrushing crises. The people, only imperfectly aware of Truman's efforts, decided on change, and the climate of the country turned against the Democrats. In 1946 the party lost control of Congress for the first time since 1930. The subsequent Republican-dominated Congress, the 80th, was even less inclined to enact the domestic legislation that Truman asked of it.

But if Truman was often frustrated in his domestic policies, it was a different story in foreign affairs. A careful student of U. S. history, Truman had learned an important lesson: not to quarrel unnecessarily with the Senate. He would not imitate Woodrow Wilson who had fought so bitterly with Senator Henry Cabot Lodge over U.S. membership in the League of Nations in 1919. Instead Truman frequently invited Senate leaders to the White House for consultations, carefully and diligently asking their opinions. He won over eminent Republicans like Senator Arthur Vandenberg and was able to gain support for what could be called a national foreign policy. As a result, the Senate voted enormous appropriations and backed the bold policies that bulwarked war-ravaged Europe and started the "Free World" on its road to recovery.

Despite these accomplishments, Truman was on the defensive as the 1948 election approached. It was almost universally assumed that he would be beaten.

Progress in foreign affairs, serious frustrations at home

139

The assumption led to very open conspiracies within the Democratic Party to deny him the nomination, a kind of mutiny that Captain Truman had no intention of tolerating. He had his drawbacks as a politician. He was often indiscreet at press conferences, and he sometimes contradicted himself, relying too much on his memory, good as it was. He may be suspected of having succumbed to some political temptations: the very rapid U.S. recognition of the government of Israel was connected by some critics with vote-getting in the Bronx rather than with Truman's concern to bolster the new Jewish state. Truman's confidence that he could get elected never wavered, however. He coolly got the nomination in Chicago and then set out on his famous and arduous "give 'em hell" campaign. To the confusion of pundits and pollsters, he won.

By 1950 the United States had recovered from the brief postwar depression and from the brief and trivial shortages that followed the war. The fruits of Truman's decisiveness and successful moves in what was the most important part of his office, foreign affairs, soon became apparent. The Marshall Plan, a brilliantly conceived blueprint for the revitalization of European industry instead of a vengeful stripping of the conquered countries' resources, was one of the key achievements of his foreign policy. Although the makers of the Marshall Plan were such men as Dean Acheson and, above all, George Marshall, the final responsibility resided in the White House. The decision to concentrate American aid and military resources in Europe was the President's. So was the "Truman Doctrine," which probably saved Greece and Turkey from a Russian-inspired Communist upheaval. The resolve to use the "airlift" to defy Stalin's attempt to isolate Berlin was a Presidential decision. Thus Western Europe was saved from the danger of collapsing in economic chaos and misery out of which a Communist controlled Europe might well have emerged.

Meanwhile Truman was ever-more-vigorously taking hold of the job of Chief Executive. He would not brook sloppy work or any form of insubordination in his official family. When Secretary of State Byrnes overstepped his role by presuming to negotiate with the Russians without keeping Truman fully informed of his steps (he issued independent press statements and generally acted as if *he* were the country's leader), he soon found himself replaced by Marshall. The same fate befell the irascible, powerful Harold Ickes, long Roosevelt's Secretary of the Interior, when he crossed Truman.

Hindsight suggests that the President did not sufficiently allow for the fact that his bold foreign policy required more military strength than his economical administration permitted. It is often forgotten that it was Mr. Truman who, for a brief period, first balanced the budget after many years of built-in deficits. Perhaps he took this part of his job too seriously. The outbreak of the Korean War put a tremendous strain on the nation's military establishment, weakened by the cutbacks Truman had made in the interests of economy. The Korean War was a turning point in his administration, casting a shadow over its later years and over his miraculous election in 1948.

Bold and speedy intervention in Korea

The War had three results for Mr. Truman's immediate popularity and perhaps for his permanent reputation. It showed, first of all, his power of decision at its highest. Instead of giving South Korea "all kinds of aid except help," as the Washington wags predicted, President Truman immediately ordered General Douglas MacArthur to dispatch troops to support South Korea's faltering forces. He did not, as we have noted, ask for a Congressional declaration of war or, indeed, for Congressional approval. It was a pure exercise of Presidential prerogative, of a sort much criticized today because of Vietnam. But there is no doubt that President Truman was within his rights as Commander-in-Chief, although he was exercising those rights to the full.

A second result of the Korean War for Mr. Truman was his much publicized and hotly debated dismissal of General MacArthur. MacArthur openly challenged

Truman's direct orders to confine the war to Korean soil and refrain from violating China's borders. Truman asserted his authority without hesitation and relieved the general of his command. There can be little or no doubt that he was constitutionally right. No general can be allowed to openly criticize and oppose the policy of the Commander-in-Chief. Lincoln, as Truman knew from his reading, had not stood for this from General George B. McClellan, and Truman did not stand for it from a much greater soldier, Douglas MacArthur. Captain Truman knew the spirit and the letter of the American Constitution better than his five-star General of the Army.

But all of Truman's decisiveness could not bring an end to the Korean War. The fifth bloodiest conflict in American history, it dragged on and on, deeply disillusioning a country brought up to believe that all its wars ended in complete victories signalized by Yorktown, Appomattox or Tokyo Bay. It cast a pall over Mr. Truman's last years in the Presidency and doubtless influenced the 1952 election, which put a Republican in the White House. It could and should be argued that the Korean War offered America a valuable lesson in the perils and perplexities that lurk in Asia. But it was an expensive lesson, and it was only imperfectly digested. It served to confirm in their beliefs those who clung to the legend that the U. S. somehow "lost China," that only some form of negligence (or possibly treason) allowed the Communists to take over. And it has been pointed to by those who believe that every form of aggression in Asia must be met with military counterforce.

If Truman had a leading fault as Chief Executive it was that he almost invariably met problems head on—which sometimes meant that he ran his head against a Congressional stone wall. This fault, of course, is but the mirror image of his overwhelming virtue, his bold decisiveness. His legacy to the office, to the nation and to the world was great and on the whole beneficent.

"His legacy to the office, to the nation and to the world was great and on the whole beneficent"

He held the front of the "Free World" against Communism when many people believed that the front was collapsing. He defended the prerogatives of the President against an overweening general. He made the Presidency for the first time in its history an effectively organized instrument of government. He opened the Pandora's box of the atomic bomb. Perhaps it had to be opened; perhaps it had to be opened that way. Perhaps because it was opened that way it need never be opened again. No one knows.

An outstanding quality of Truman himself was his ironical acceptance of his own limitations, his humor and his dislike of pomposity. He is reported to have offered an important job to a man he much admired who demurred, saying, "I don't really feel qualified for it." Truman replied, "Maybe you're not. There are probably hundreds of people better qualified than you, but I don't know any of them. There are probably hundreds of people better qualified than I am to be President, but they weren't elected." Whether Truman really believed the second half of this famous statement is doubtful. What is certain is that he never acted as if the task of being President was an easy one, that it demanded anything less than his never-flagging zeal and constant watchfulness. It was this quality perhaps more than any other that made him the very remarkable and possibly great President that he was.

And—a point very hard to demonstrate, but which it is necessary to make— he showed in his brisk, man-in-the-street, man-from-the-farm way that the promise of American life for the average citizen had not been withdrawn. It has been an age of Presidents whose backgrounds have been very different from that of Harry Truman: a great engineer, Hoover; a country gentleman full of the social arts, F.D.R.; a great soldier, Eisenhower; a great millionaire with charm, high culture, dazzling personal appearance, Kennedy. The American public, as it rejoiced in his upset victory of 1948, took and kept to its heart the brusque little man from Independence, Missouri.

IN MEMORIAM
Harry S. Truman
1884-1972

The flag in the front yard of the Truman home in
Independence, Missouri, was lowered to half-staff
when news of the former President's death reached
the Truman family. The former President passed
away early December 26th.

Mrs. Bess Truman (right) and her daughter
Mrs. Margaret Truman Daniel walk together as
they leave the Truman home to go to the funeral
home.

*"He was a builder in a world ravished by war. He was
a healer in a world beset by disease, pestilence and
poverty. He was a giant of a man who lived in troubled
times and had the courage to make difficult decisions."*
Senator Hubert H. Humphrey

The route of the motocade passed the Truman house where all of the shades were drawn except one from which Mrs. Truman, exhausted by the long vigil, watched.

"His word was always good."
Cyrus Eaton, Director of the Truman Library

"He was a man of tremendous courage. I feel that history will record him as one of our truly great presidents."
Governor George Wallace

"His place in history is secure; he stands tall among world leaders."
Vice-President Spiro T. Agnew

"A very honest man, a very brave man."
Arnold Toynbee

The casket containing the body of former President Harry S. Truman is followed by his daughter and members of her family as it is carried from the funeral home enroute to the Harry S. Truman Library.

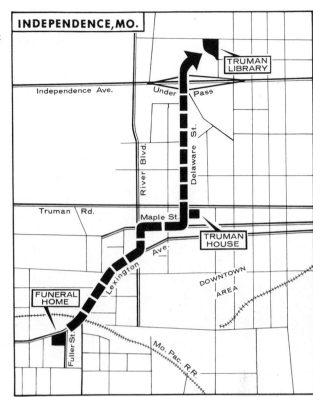

President Truman's daughter, Margaret Truman Daniel, and her family (at left) look on as the casket containing the body of former President Harry S. Truman is placed in the lobby of the Truman Library on the morning of December 27 to lie in state.

"The world is a better place for his having lived in it."
General of the Army Omar N. Bradley

"He was a fighter, who was at his best when the going was toughest. He will be remembered as one of the most courageous presidents in our history."
President Richard Nixon

"A 20th-century giant is gone. I shall be grateful all my days for the privilege of having known so great a man."
Former President Lyndon Baines Johnson

"Harry Truman was a great liberal, a great progressive, a truly courageous man."
AFL-CIO President George Meany

Thomas Hart Benton, a close friend of former President Truman, wipes a tear from his eye as the casket lies in state before the mural he painted for the Truman Library years before.

President Nixon and his wife, Pat, walk past the casket of former President Truman and bid farewell to the man from Independence, Missouri.

Former President Lyndon Baines Johnson (center left) bows his head as he and his family view the casket of Harry S. Truman. Standing with Lyndon Johnson are (left to right) Charles and Linda Robb, Lady Bird Johnson, and Luci and Pat Nugent.

Early on the morning of December 28, the former President's many friends and neighbors waited in line to pay their last respects. Seventy-five thousand men, women and children—rich and poor, famous and unknown—filed slowly and silently by his mahogany casket in final tribute.

"The Greek people bestow Harry Truman with sentiments of deep gratitude and will always honor the memory of this great son of the American people."
Premier George Papadopoulos

"I always admired his integrity, his judgment and the foreign policy he inspired."
George Bidault, French Foreign Minister

"We mourn a statesman who courageously committed himself to the defense of freedom. The memory of American President Harry S. Truman will always remain alive in Germany."
West German Chancellor Willy Brandt

"The American people have lost a great leader and we have lost one of the greatest and most faithful friends of Israel."
The Israeli Knesset (Parliament)

Ending the graveside funeral service, Fifth Army Commander Lt. Gen. Patrick Cassidy (left) presents Mrs. Bess Truman with the flag that had draped her husband's casket throughout the services. Behind them are Mr. and Mrs. Clifton Daniel, Mrs. Truman's daughter and son-in-law. Former President Truman was buried quietly as he had wished and in a spot he himself had selected, in the grassy courtyard of the Truman Library.

INDEX *Numerals in italics indicate an illustration of the subject mentioned.*

CREDITS

The sources for the illustrations in this book are shown below. Credits for the pictures from left to right are separated by commas, from top to bottom by dashes.

CHAPTER 1: 6—James Whitmore for LIFE. 10, 11—James Whitmore for LIFE, Thomas D. McAvoy for LIFE. 12—Thomas D. McAvoy for LIFE. 13—Thomas D. McAvoy for LIFE—Peter Stackpole for LIFE. 14, 15—Anthony Linck for LIFE, map by Jerome Kuhl. 16—James Whitmore for LIFE—Thomas D. McAvoy for LIFE. 17—Peter Stackpole for LIFE. 18—Cartoon by Barrow in the Rochester *Democrat & Chronicle* © Culver Pictures, W. Eugene Smith for LIFE, James Whitmore for LIFE, Joe Scherschel for LIFE—Peter Stackpole for LIFE. 20—Francis Miller for LIFE. 21—Thomas D. McAvoy for LIFE. 23—Charles Farr from Graphic House for LIFE—CBS Photo-Urgo—Jack Brinton. 24, 25—W. Eugene Smith for LIFE.

CHAPTER 2: 26—Brown Brothers. 28, 29—Eliot Elisofon for LIFE—Culver Pictures. 30, 31—European Picture Service. 32, 33—United Press International. 34—Alfred Eisenstaedt from Pix for LIFE. 35—Eliot Elisofon for LIFE. 36, 37—United Press International, Mary Ethel Noland. 39—United Press International. 40, 41—J. L. Williams for the Kansas City *Star Times*, United Press International. 42, 43—Map by Robert N. Essman, U.S. Signal Corps. 45—Wide World Photos.

CHAPTER 3: 48—United Press International, Alfred Eisenstaedt from Pix for LIFE. 52, 53—United Press International except top the Kansas City *Star Times*. 54—Paul Dorsey for LIFE. 55—Thomas D. McAvoy for LIFE. 56, 57—Thomas D. McAvoy for LIFE, Edmund B. Gerard for LIFE. 58, 59—George Skadding for LIFE—Edmund B. Gerard for LIFE, Thomas D. McAvoy for LIFE. 60, 61—United Press International, Harris and Ewing. 62, 63—George Skadding for LIFE.

CHAPTER 4: 64—Edward Clark for LIFE. 68, 69—Edward Clark for LIFE. 70—United Press International. 71—Marie Hansen for LIFE. 72—Bob Landry for LIFE—Alfred Eisenstaedt from Pix for LIFE. 73—Wide World Photos—Leonard McCombe for LIFE. 74, 75—Nat Farbman for LIFE, Thomas D. McAvoy for LIFE, Gjon Mili for LIFE—Joe Scherschel for LIFE. 76, 77—Wide World Photos. 78, 79—William Belknap Jr. from Rapho Guillumette. 80, 81—U.S. Air Force—Bernard Hoffman for LIFE. 82—United Press International, Francis Miller for LIFE. 83—Thomas D. McAvoy for LIFE, Fenno Jacobs for FORTUNE. 84—Marie Hansen for LIFE. 85—Cartoon reprint from *The Tampa Tribune*—Wide World Photos. 86, 87—Allan Grant from Graphic House for LIFE.

88, 89—John Zimmerman for TIME except right Marie Hansen for LIFE. 90, 91—United Press International. 92—Cartoon by C. D. Batchelor © New York *Daily News*—cartoon by Packer © New York Daily *Mirror* reprinted with permission from Hearst Newspapers. 93—Cartoon by Packer © New York Daily *Mirror* reprinted with permission from Hearst Newspapers, cartoon by Seibel © *Richmond Times-Dispatch* —cartoon by Dorman H. Smith © Newspaper Enterprise Association, cartoon by H. I. Carlisle reprinted with permission from the Des Moines *Register and Tribune*, cartoon by Hutton © *The Philadelphia Inquirer*—cartoon by Hank Barrow reprinted with permission from the *Omaha World Herald*, cartoon by Cecil Jensen reprinted with permission from the *Chicago Daily News*.

CHAPTER 5: 94—Mark Kauffman for LIFE. 96, 97—United Press International, Thomas D. McAvoy for LIFE, George Skadding for LIFE. 98—the Kansas City *Star Times*. 99—Yale Joel for LIFE. 100—George Skadding for LIFE except left Thomas D. McAvoy for LIFE—Werner Stoy from Camera Hawaii. 101—William Belknap Jr. from Rapho Guillumette, Carl Mydans for LIFE, Official U.S. Navy Photo—United Press International, Polifoto Press Service, Harris and Ewing. 102, 103—United Press International. 104, 105—Wide World Photos except top left Walter Bennett for TIME. 106, 107—Bottom left Wide World Photos. 108, 109—Alfred Eisenstaedt for LIFE, Wide World Photos.

CHAPTER 6: 110—Wide World Photos. 112—Hank Walker for LIFE, United Press International. 114—David Douglas Duncan for LIFE. 115—Al Chang for U.S. Signal Corps. 116, 117—Map by Robert Essman, George Skadding for LIFE. 118, 119—Cartoon by Herblock from *The Herblock Book* (Beacon Press, 1951), John Dominis for LIFE. 120, 121—United Press International except top left Hank Walker for LIFE.

CHAPTER 7: 122, 123—Eliot Elisofon for LIFE. 124, 125—Alfred Eisenstaedt from Pix for LIFE, Eliot Elisofon for LIFE—Grey Villet for LIFE. 126, 127—Grey Villet for LIFE except bottom left Alfred Eisenstaedt for LIFE. 128—Frank Scherschel for LIFE—Cornell Capa for LIFE. 129—Jim Mahan for LIFE. 130—Carl Mydans for LIFE. 131 —Paris *Match*. 132, 133—United Press International. 134, 135—Harry S. Truman Library photo—Frank Scherschel for LIFE, Robert W. Kelley for LIFE. 136—United Press International.

IN MEMORIAM—All photos and text materials supplied through the courtesy of United Press International